STOP WORRYING AND ANXIETY

HOW TO REPLACE STRESS AND NEGATIVE THINKING WITH HAPPINESS, MINDFULNESS, AND POSITIVE THINKING

JONATHAN GREEN

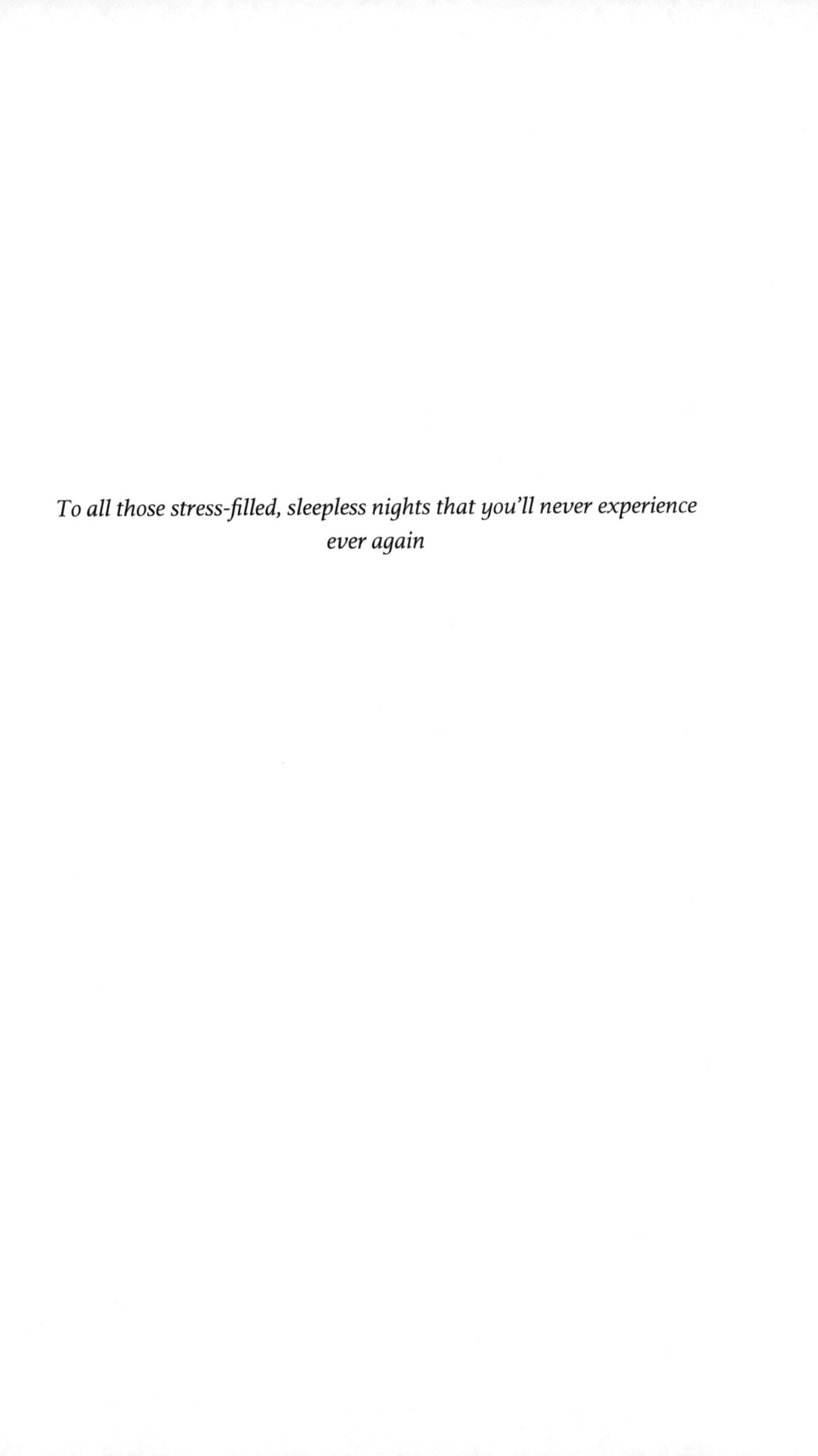

*To all those stress-filled, sleepless nights that you'll never experience
ever again*

FREE GIFT

ServeNoMaster.com/worrygroup

Thank you for your purchase of *Stop Worry and Anxiety*. As an extra bonus, I want to give you a free gift.

We have a special and amazing group of entrepreneurs and authors who have all been where you are right now.

Having a group of people around you who understand depression, anxiety, and stress is the BEST way to stay the course and overcome your problem.

With our support your success becomes inevitable.

Don't wait to finish the book, we are ready to spend time with you RIGHT NOW.

Accelerate your success and click the link below to get instant access:

ServeNoMaster.com/worrygroup

1

ARE YOU A WORRIER?

We live in a world filled with massive amounts of stress. We hear about it every day. If it's not in the newspaper, you'll see a report on television about stress being a silent killer, linked to most of the top-ten causes of death in America. Stress is the hidden factor behind high blood pressure, heart attacks, strokes, and even some forms of cancer. We know that this monster is a killer, and yet the more we hear about it, the worse it gets.

For most of us, hearing about stress and all of the problems it causes makes the situation worse and stresses us out even more. In this book, we aren't going to focus on all of the bad signs of stress, all of the negatives. We know that stress is bad for you; we know that worry and anxiety are bad for you.

Together, we are going to work on how to conquer them, and by the end of this book, you'll have the tools to understand exactly how to overcome the causes of your anxiety and lower your stress levels – how to feel like you are back in control of your emotional and spiritual side. It is important to maintain a balance between your physical, mental, spiritual, and artistic sides. In this book, we are focusing on those key components: your mental and spiritual sides, which are the parts of you most vulnerable to stress.

Before we get started, please take the brief quiz below. It's a test to check whether you are a big worrier and where exactly you are on the spectrum. Knowing where we started is very important at the end; you can take the quiz again to see how you have progressed and, of course, you can take it again further down the line and watch how you improve.

Are You a Worrier Assessment?

1. Do you ever feel anxious for no apparent reason?
    a) Yes, I do quite often.
    b) Only occasionally.

2. Do you ever experience insomnia?
    a) Yes.
    b) Very occasionally, or never.

3. How DIFFICULT do you find it to deal with anxious thoughts?
    a) Very difficult.
    b) Somewhat difficult, or not difficult.

4. How DIFFICULT do you find it to live completely in the moment, and not worry in any way about the past or future?
    a) Usually very difficult.
    b) Somewhat difficult, or not difficult.

5. ARE you prone to very negative thinking?
    a) Yes.
    b) Not really, or no.

6. Do you tend to catastrophize (expect the worst-case scenario)?
   a) Yes.
   b) No.

SCORING: THE MORE "A" answers you chose, the more of a worrier you are.

If you scored very high on this quiz, fear not. Having a larger problem means that the change in your life will be more significant. Each exercise in this book will bring you more relief than you ever thought possible.

If you are at the low end of the spectrum, you might not notice massive changes in your life with each exercise, but your overall journey to a stress-free living will be shorter!

Characteristics of Anxiety

Sometimes, we don't even realize what we are dealing with, and we can misdiagnose ourselves. People hop online and search for the meaning of their combination of symptoms, and often end up with an incorrect diagnosis. Some of them think that signs that you're suffering from chronic anxiety or a long-term problem or they have uncontrollable and excessive worry.

You have a chronic problem if you feel like you are always worried about something, and when one worry goes away you replace it with a new one; you can't ever live fully in the moment, and you feel like the back of your mind is thinking about something else – for instance, you are talking to someone, but all you can think about is your worries and the chores you have to take care of later.

You may also notice some physical symptoms. When I'm worried or nervous, my heartbeat starts to accelerate and my pulse increases.

How often do you notice your heart racing, beating harder and faster?

Sometimes you might notice that you're having palpitations when you are beginning to have a full-on panic attack. In these moments of acute stress, you may notice that your skin gets very hot, or you feel sick to your stomach like you are going to throw up. That feeling of butterflies in your stomach that turns from cute pre-stage jitters to feeling like the butterflies are going to rip out of your torso and flood all over the stage. As your stress levels rise, you may begin to feel more physical symptoms; you might experience constant headaches, have difficulty thinking, and even trouble sleeping.

A major cause of insomnia is that you can't stop worrying about things; you're lying in bed, and you want to sleep, but all you can think about is the sources of your worry, and they have become over-whelming. It's hard for you to relax. It's like a movie scene where the stressed-out person tries yoga or meditation. They look very relaxed, but as soon as the camera zooms into that person's head, you can hear what they're thinking, feeling completely terrified and stressed out. The meditation isn't working because they're not able to focus on it at all. Their mind isn't in the moment, they can't stay calm, they can't become relaxed; they can't leave the anxious state.

Lastly, you might just feel a bit of an overwhelming malaise. A fear of anxiety or just a generalized fear, like you never feel totally relaxed or at ease, almost as though you are perpetually waiting for the other shoe to drop.

Exercise

This is a cooperative book. It is not a book full of trite sayings and cute lines you can memorize. This is a book of action, and I would like you to join me on this journey.

Get a notebook: it is going to be your Worry and Anxiety Journal. If you prefer, you can use a computer file instead. I'm a big believer in physical notebooks; I like writing my notes out by hand, but if you are listening to an audiobook and taking notes on your phone, you have that option too, but please find a way to take notes as you work through the activities. We are going to start with some reflection questions right now.

Reflection Questions

1. Before starting this book, how would you rate yourself as a worrier on a scale of one to ten? Were you surprised by the results of the first worry-assessment quiz?

2. How severe does your worrying problem feel? Do you have moments of relaxation sometimes, or do you have moments of intense stress, anxiety, and paranoia? Take time to describe how you feel in detail; the more you describe what you are feeling, the easier it will be to overcome that feeling.

3. How has worrying altered or affected your life? Has it affected your career? Has it affected any of your relationships? How has it damaged those areas of your life?

4. Do you have other friends who are worriers? Do you have people in your life who worry as much or more than you do? Looking at their experience of being an anxious or worrying person from the outside, what do you notice about their experience? What do you notice about someone who spends so much of their time being worried? How has worrying affected their lives?

5. Look at the list of the characteristics of anxiety in the section above. How many of those characteristics apply to you? How many of them do you suffer from, but hadn't thought about before? Are there any parts of your anxiety that weren't on the list? Write down anything that was on the list as part of your personal experience. Which is the primary symptom of all the different characteristics and results of anxiety and worrying? Which one is affecting your life the most? Which one drove you to purchase this book?

6. Mindfulness is the practice of living completely in the present moment and not letting worries about the past or the future occupy your mind. How good are you at practicing mindfulness? Do you want to improve in this area?

7. How do you feel that a better level of mindfulness will help you in your journey to worrying less and experiencing less anxiety?

8. How soon do you begin to worry about something? Does it transition into anxiety to start to experience the symptoms we talked

about above? Which symptoms of anxiety come first? Does it start with headaches? Does it start with a racing heart or with a feeling of fear? What do your first symptoms lead to?

9. What would your life be like without anxiety, without worrying anymore? This is a longer answer. Describe what it would be like to go through a day in your ideal life, with no more worries.

Exercise

A great deal of worrying's power comes from how we respond passively. It's time to become active. The next time you notice you start to worry about something, become very conscious of your experience. You have your Worry and Anxiety Journal with you. Write down exactly what's happening, the time, the date, and what you worried about. Try to isolate the cause of your worry. Was it just a stray thought? Did someone say something at work? Did you hear something on the radio or see something on television? We often have triggers for worry that we're not even conscious of. We want to start to isolate them.

In your Journal, write down whether your worry was rational or irrational. Certain things are reasonable to worry about, and certain things are not. Be honest with yourself; no one else is going to see your Journal.

Next, analyze your negative thinking. In your Journal, write down your key negative thoughts and why they were irrational, what was wrong with them. You want to begin to challenge your negative thinking, and this means you are going to take an objective stance when you have your negative thoughts. Anxiety and fear are very emotional experiences; it can be very hard to be objective when you're in an emotional state.

The best way to do this is to close your eyes and imagine that you're a psychiatrist or counselor, and someone comes in and describes the exact symptoms you're experiencing. Through looking at it objectively, you can assess their situation. When looking at this imaginary patient's problem rationally and objectively. Does their worry seem reasonable or unreasonable? When we can switch from the worry state into the calm, objective analysis state, much of the worry will disappear. This is the first of many powerful techniques we will discuss in this book.

2

____

CAUSES OF ANXIETY

Worry and stress can grow and become more powerful. Anxiety is what we call "chronic." There are many different causes of stress in your life; we want to begin to isolate those particular stressors to find out what your triggers are. This is why we are going to write down every time you have a worrying attack – its cause and what you experience.

For now, let's do a quick analysis to find your current stress level. Complete this stress-level test to see where you are on the spectrum.

Stress Level Test

1. Are you able to take quiet time purely for yourself every day?
    a) Rarely or never.
    b) Yes.

2. Is your income high enough to cover your basic expenses?
    a) No.
    b) Yes.

3. Do you usually feel in control of your day?
　a) No.
　b) Yes.

4. Do you have at least one full, hot meal every day?
　a) No.
　b) Yes.

5. Do you sleep at least seven or eight hours a night, four or more nights each week?
　a) No.
　b) Yes, usually.

SCORING: THE MORE "A" answers you have, the higher your stress level is.

How Can You Reduce the Effects of Stress on Your Life?

You know that stress is bad for you, otherwise you wouldn't be reading this book. The last thing you want is ten chapters all about how stress is bad. Rather than harping on the negative, we are going to jump right to the solution. How can you reduce your stress levels?

You may feel like stress is inevitable or it's an overwhelming force, but in fact, it's something very manageable, and together we can take action to minimize stress in your life.

1. EXERCISE MORE OFTEN. There is a direct connection between your psychology and your physiology: the state of your body affects the state of your mind, and vice versa. When I go more than three days without exercising, my anxiety and stress levels begin to rise. I know that anxiety is a powerful force. If your first thought was, "This is

some trite advice about exercise," that's a sign that you definitely need to get physical, and that your stress is affecting your decision-making.

Stress can build up in your body in the form of chemicals and hormones. Our bodies were designed to be active; they were not designed to sit at a computer and type all day. Recent studies have shown that simply sitting for your job can increase the chances of high blood pressure and heart attack.

You've heard of the exercise nightmare – what you imagine in your mind is something horrible, like working with a personal trainer who will shout at you all the time, or going to the gym and doing exercises that you hate, surrounded by beautiful people quickly mocking you with hands over their mouths. The very thought of this type of exercise is stressful.

Instead, we want to find a sport or activity that is physical and you enjoy, depending on your current health level. Find an activity that involves doing something that you love. Whether it's going for hikes, joining a nature photography club, getting into geocaching (which is where you walk around and use different GPS coordinates to find treasures) – there a lot of activities that you can add to your life, even if you have physical limitations.

We want to focus more on sport and exercise. For me, sports are fun; exercises are not. I struggle to go to the gym and lift weights. It's very hard for me to want to do that, but I can have a twenty-five-minute yoga lesson and really enjoy it. Getting in my kayak and paddling around, getting on my paddleboard, and doing anything in the ocean is how I relieve my stress.

Your first thought might be, "He's got it so easy; he lives on the beach. It's easy for him to limit stress." You have to realize I moved here because of my stress. I moved to the beach because I was over-weight and unhealthy, and I know that this is an environment where it's easier to get rid of stress. I wanted to make it easier for me to exercise harder, so moving to the beach was an active decision to help me deal with my weight, health problems, and stress levels.

Even without doing beach activities in the morning, I often do a yoga DVD. I'm a big fan of good yoga programs that are short. I like to do twenty to twenty-five minutes because even with a busy workday, I can set aside that amount of time. That's how long most people spend driving to and from the gym. I get more done in my little window of time than most people do going to the gym and doing something they hate.

Think about getting physical and think about doing something fun; the more fun your activity is, the better. There are a lot of great websites about doing fun physical activities in your community. Look up the adult learning centers and sports leagues. Did you know that most cities and even small towns now have sports that they organize? If you're doing something fun, the rest of it becomes very easy.

2. CHOOSE A HEALTHIER DIET. The key to choosing a healthier diet is finding something that you can maintain. Most diets fail because they are about action change. "Stop eating this. You cannot eat that." If we focus instead on foods that lower anxiety versus raising your anxiety, then we'll begin to change how we think about food. Consider your limitations, and when you think of diet, I want you to imagine something you can maintain for the rest of your life. Most diets are hard because they're extreme, and they begin to feel like a curse. Find a diet that you can maintain for a long time.

When I say diet, I mean eating lifestyle. My diet is primarily Thai food and Paleo, a low-carb regime. If you want a very simple diet, I'll share mine with you. I don't eat any grains, and I only drink water. These two changes really make a difference. I don't eat dairy, so no cheese or ice cream. I don't eat white grains, which include potatoes, rice, and bread. I don't put calories into my body in the form of drinks. These changes are easy to maintain in a diet.

When I buy cookbooks, I like to buy Paleo cookbooks, as I know I can eat everything in there. Thai is a very healthy Asian diet. In the West, Chinese food is turned into deep-frying everything, covering it in MSG, and adding a sauce. I prefer a lighter touch, which I find in

Thai books. All you have to do is find a diet that you can easily maintain.

3. AVOID UNNECESSARY STRESS. There are certain things in life that we have to do. We have to go to school as children, and as adults, we go to work to pay our bills. These are all stressful things. As you work through your Journal, write down each time you feel anxiety, stress, and worry entering your life. Look for triggers you can remove.

One of my big causes of anxiety was politics. I used to read a lot of news websites because I wanted to know everything that was going on in the world, but I don't do it anymore. My life hasn't changed at all other than lowering my anxiety levels. Whether you're on the left or the right, the news is designed to keep you in a perpetual state of anxiety, so you keep watching more. It's addictive, and it is a for-profit business. Their goal is to get as many people watching as possible to sell as many commercials as possible. The news is not altruistic. In the local newspaper, there are only two things that will affect your life: the movie listings and the weather. The rest of it won't alter what you do today.

Find those stress triggers in your life that you don't need. Do you have a friend who always gives you stress? When I was younger, I had a friend who became my trigger – always making me feel bad about myself. After a while, I noticed I liked hanging out with them, but then when I got home, I would always feel worse about myself. He was affecting my self-esteem. Every time I hung out with him, I'd come home feeling fatter and uglier than I did when I left. I did not want to do that anymore, so I stopped spending time with him, and I started feeling better about myself.

Find your triggers and begin to remove them. If you have a manager at work who is constantly stressing you out, try to spend more time with another manager or try to design ways to avoid the stressful moments.

4. **Distinguish between what you can and cannot change.** There are things in life that we have no power over. I can't control the weather. I can't control politics. I can't control what other people say, do, or think. These are things that I cannot change, and I accept them. If there is something in your life that's worrying you, but you cannot control it, sit down and say to yourself, "There is nothing I can do to change the situation. This person will always be this way. This problem will always be there." It will begin to take the sting out of that stressor and help you accept the things that you can't change.

5. **Reframe your problems.** Reframing is one of the most powerful techniques in the world, and the best example of reframing I've ever seen is in the movie *300*. My favorite line from that movie is one of the Persians saying to one of the Spartans, "We are going to shoot so many arrows into the sky that it will block the sun." And the Spartan responds, "Great, then we'll get to fight in the shade." This is the ultimate reframing; they took the worst thing someone can say to you and reframed it as a positive. The more we can find the positive and the benefit in things in our lives, the easier they become to deal with.

One of the greatest stresses in my life was a terrible relationship that I was in between the ages of twenty-five and twenty-seven. I had an "on-again, off-again" relationship with a girl that ended in disaster. I have written about this terrible relationship in other books.

She left me so damaged that I couldn't be in the same country as her. That relationship is the reason that I moved to England, and it began my transformative journey. I wouldn't be where I am right now if that relation hadn't been so bad; I wouldn't have become an author. I see it as one of the best things ever happened to me. It was so bad it forced me to change my life for the better. Even the worst experiences in life can lead to great things.

6. **Look at the bigger picture.** When you're in the moment, and you're feeling stressed about something, look at things in perspective.

This advice can feel very unpleasant, but the truth is, there's always someone out there who's got it worse than you. People love to complain online about their problems, their anxiety, and their stressors. Oftentimes, we look at these things they post online and say, "How can you even be stressed about that?"

I went through great stress recently, when my wife was having issues with her pregnancy. We spent two weeks in the hospital, fighting and doing everything we could, and we finally came home. Everything seemed fine, but we lost the child two days later to miscarriage. This was very painful and stressful for us, and it's a worse experience than most people have. But I have friends who've lost a living child, and that is even more painful – it's every parent's nightmare.

Even though I was in a situation much worse than most people, I was still aware that other people have experienced worse things than me. Many of the things that people complain about and call their stressors are things that my wife laughs at with disdain.

My wife has fought multiple wild animals for survival when she was a child. The first time she fought a wild animal for her life she was six years old. We don't have that in the West. We don't even know what it's like to live in a world where a wild animal can kill you. In fact, an animal killed one of her sisters when she was a baby. My wife knows what it's like to starve; she knows what it's like to go to the bathroom in the woods every day, when you can't afford a toilet or water or electricity. When you look at your problems in perspective, they become smaller.

7. **REACH out to people you can depend on.** Having a group of people around you who bring you up rather than down can be very powerful. When you're suffering from acute stress, you can do some activities that help you break through. I talk about this in some of my other books. I'm a big fan of the batting cages because it's fun and it's a physical activity. It doesn't feel like it, but the next day your arms will be hurting. You don't have to impress anyone by hitting major

6. Which of these techniques do you find the most exciting? Which technique do you look forward to trying out? Why?

7. Which of these stress management techniques do you think will be the most challenging? Why?

8. What actions are you going to take to ensure your success with improving these techniques and managing your stress?

9. How can you reward yourself for conquering your stress in the moment and hitting your exercise goal? Develop a structure where you reward yourself mentally or with a small treat that helps you to stay in a positive mindset.

3

HOW WORRYING AND ANXIETY CAN NEGATIVELY AFFECT YOUR LIFE

Stress, worrying, and anxiety can all affect your life in negative ways, both physically and mentally. They can begin to feel overwhelming. Some of the results of stress that we will discuss in this chapter are probably very familiar to you and may be the very reason that you purchased this book. Certain stresses in life are unavoidable, but we can minimize the effect of stress on your life.

Real versus Imaginary Fear

Most of the things that we worry about are not real. We worry about things in the future and from the past that are never going to happen in real life.

Real fear is when a tiger is in the room with me; if I'm locked in a cage with a tiger, I should be afraid. If I don't have a weapon, the odds of me winning a fight with a tiger are very slim. That's a real and legitimate reason to be afraid. If I am worried that a tiger might attack me, but I'm sitting on the bus, that's imaginary; it's not real. That's worry, rather than fear. Imaginary worries, real fears.

Take a moment to assess how worries are affecting your life. Are you worried about things that are absolutely imaginary? When we are living in the moment, when we are practicing a state of mindfulness, these worries will disappear.

Imaginary worry activates a fight or flight reflex and releases stress hormones. These hormones release energy into our body to either fight or run away in an emergency. The process itself is healthy, and it's what your body is designed for. That's how the human race has continued to survive despite the fact that we have experienced many animal attacks throughout our history. But when we are in that state of emergency for long periods of time, the effects become very unhealthy, and acute stress can turn into chronic stress.

When you start to feel worried about something, stop for a moment and think, "Is this real or imaginary?" It's easy to say that there's a good chance what you're worried about will happen, but that's a sign that you're giving too much power to your worry. If it's not happening right now, don't worry about it – don't let it affect your emotions or activate a stressful state.

The Reverse Worry

I used to be a big worrier, and I used to be very creative about all the different things that could happen and all the different ways I could die. Then, twenty years ago, I read an article saying that ninety percent of the things we worry about never happen. As I began to look at the things I was worried about, I realized none of them ever came true.

Write down in your Worry and Anxiety Journal the ten biggest things you have worried about in the past. Look back at the main things you worried about in high school, in college, or in your twenties. Were you worried that you would never find a job? Or you were never going to move out of your parent's house? Or you were never going to have a relationship? How many of those things that you were worried about do you still think about now? I don't need you to rely on me second-hand telling you that ninety percent of the things we worry about will never happen. I want you to experience this by looking at your own history.

When I began to look at the things I worry and how often they come true, I realized I'm a terrible predictor. If I worry about something, I know that means it probably won't happen. Adding this technique to your life will really help you. When I become anxious about something, I realize that it probably won't happen. That immediately shuts down the cause of my worry. I realize that it's an imaginary worry and not a real fear. Anytime I've attempted to predict the future, I have absolutely failed. Look at your own ability to predict via worrying. How many of the things you were worried about were a total waste of time? Have you *ever* worried about something that eventually came true?

Experience Takes Away the Sting

You may have a few experiences in your life where you were worried about something and it happened. I want you to be honest and write this down in your Worry and Anxiety Journal. When you worried about something, and then it happened, was the experience as bad as you thought it was going to be?

When I was younger, I was terrified of talking women. I was terrified of being embarrassed in public, and I was always afraid to talk to strangers. I suffered from a great deal of social anxiety. I went through very long periods in which I had no one in my life. I had no friends, no one to talk to, and I suffered greatly.

When I was twenty-seven, I decided I wanted to change my life, and someone who's very much my life right now has helped me through this time. He said, "I want you to walk across this bar, talk to those women, and get them to reject you," and he pointed to two women who were older than me. I said, "What? That sounds weird." He said, "I want you to experience what you're actually afraid of, and see what it's like." I went over and had this conversation. It was very hard, but I walked away from the experience, and I realized it wasn't as bad as I thought it was going to be; my imagination was far worse than the real thing. I've experienced bad stuff in my life, and what I've learned is that I'm capable of dealing with it – and you are too.

If the things that you worry about actually happen, you will be able to deal with them. That's why you don't need to worry. When they happen, your emergency mode activates, and you handle the situation in a way you never thought possible.

Negative Physical Effects of Worrying and Anxiety

Below are some of the negative physical effects of worrying and anxiety:

- Reduced sleep
- Unhealthy habits, such as smoking and excessive drinking
- Excessive stress hormones, like cortisol, released by the nervous system
- Stress hormones increase levels of triglycerides (blood fats) and blood sugar levels
- Shortness of breath
- Rapid breathing
- Nausea
- Muscle aches and tension
- Fatigue
- Headaches
- Racing heartbeat
- Dizziness
- Swallowing difficulty

In the long run, these problems become more likely as well:

- Short-term memory loss
- Disorders of the digestive system
- Compromised immune system

- Heart disease
- Heart attack

Negative Psychological and Social Effects of Worrying and Anxiety

Worrying and anxiety are insidious; they get into your mind, and they begin to affect the way you think. This can lead to dangerous cycles. I want you to isolate the cycles in your life. How do you magnify your worry? Let me give you a couple of examples to understand what I'm talking about.

Example 1. You're stressed about work tomorrow, which leads you to have trouble sleeping tonight because you're thinking about work. You're stressed out because you're worried you won't get everything done. You go to the office the next day, and you are tired because you didn't sleep all night, so you have trouble performing. You manifested your own fear. You created a self-fulfilling prophecy. You predicted a bad day, and then you made it happen.

Example 2. When you're in meetings or doing business with other people, you get nervous that you'll mess up or say the wrong thing, or that they'll get aggressive. Because of your worries, you don't perform at your best, and you end up with inferior deals. This is why most people hire lawyers or external people to negotiate for them; it's because they get stuck in this moment. For a long time, I have thought that tough guys are good negotiators. I used to know someone who was a real tough talker, but every time I was there when he was selling something or making a negotiation, I realized he was terrible at it.

Sometimes, we can cause ourselves medical problems. We start to get worried about work that makes us feel sick, we go to the doctor, get more stressed, and we end up in this cycle. The doctor can only diagnose you based on what you tell them, so they'll start to think you have a serious problem, they'll give you medication to deal with it, and the cycle will get worse and worse. Once the doctor puts you on a medication, you feel justified in your worrying, and you've now developed a stronger sense of worry. Now you feel like you're always right when you worry. I've been through several of these myself – I've had quite a few mystery illnesses in my life that were caused by depression, stress, and anxiety.

When anxiety is affecting us, we make poor and limiting decisions. If you don't feel like you're in control of your mental health – if you feel like you're worried all the time – you'll feel like you're not a great worker, which will keep you from applying for better jobs, and this, in turn, means you'll make less money. Less money means more money stress, more money fights at home, and it gets into a cycle.

I know many people who have an imaginary glass ceiling above them, whether it's in their self-belief or financial areas. We have these invisible barriers that limit us and only exist in our own imagination. Many times in my life, I made career choices other people said were impossible. Their lack of belief has them making the same money they were making when they said my idea was impossible, while I've gone far past them. When you begin to overcome worry and anxiety, when you break out of your cycles, you are going to experience other rewards beyond feeling better all the time.

Reflection Questions

Let's complete some reflection questions on the negative effects of anxiety on your life. Write your answers in your Worry and Anxiety Journal.

1. In what ways do you feel that anxiety has negatively affected your physical well-being? Are you surprised by these effects?

2. In what ways do you feel that anxiety has negatively affected your psychological well-being? Are you surprised by these effects?

3. In what ways do you feel that anxiety has negatively affected you socially? Are you surprised by these effects?

4. How many of the effects that we have listed in this chapter have you experienced yourself?

5. Does it surprise you that anxiety has so many potential negative effects?

6. Do you feel that your culture ignores or dismisses the effects of anxiety, and blames the victim? If you agree, give some examples of where you have noticed this happening.

7. Do you feel that social stigma prevents people from admitting that they have a problem with anxiety? How damaging do you feel this stigma can be?

8. Has social stigma ever stopped you from discussing your worry or anxiety?

Exercise

The next time you feel a wave of anxiety, try to isolate the first warning signs. Try to learn how your body warns you that an anxiety cycle is starting. Maybe you notice a physical symptom, like a headache, or maybe you start to feel a little bit of depression. How do you cycle when you're in one of those moments? I want you to be very proactive and write down your experience in your Journal.

Look at whatever you are worrying about and say to yourself, "The fact that I am worrying about this means there's a ninety percent chance it will not happen."

Look at what you're worrying about and say, "Is this an imaginary worry or real fear? Is there a tiger in the room with me or am I thinking about going to the zoo tomorrow?"

Focus on achieving a state of mindfulness and on locking yourself in the moment. Focus on the here and now – what you can see, what you can smell, what you can taste. In your Journal, write down how using these three techniques helps you or doesn't help you. What was your experience? How far did you get to the techniques before you got stuck? What were your successes and what were your failures? Not everything works on the very first try. That's okay, and that's why this is a longer book; we're not at the end yet. We still have a lot to talk about.

The more you track your progress along this journey, the better.

We started with the baseline about your stress and anxiety levels and as we move forward through this book, the more you write about your experiences, the more you will have a solid record of your happiness going up and your stress levels going down. We want to track those things, so please be proactive; if you do these activities you'll notice a big change in your life.

4

GETTING INTO THE HABIT OF POSITIVE THINKING

Worrying, depression, and anxiety are all manifestations of negative thought patterns. If we can replace our negative thoughts with positive ones, we can push these bad thoughts further and further away from our minds. Anxiety cannot coexist with positive thoughts and happiness. Only one thought can dominate at a given time. Thoughts are emotions, and emotions are thoughts. Have you ever been able to experience two emotions at the same time? Have you ever been happy-sad or angry-tired?

Sometimes you have a small merging, but you're never excited-worried; they are too different. One will always be the dominant force.

As we move forward, take this quick quiz to see if you're a negative thinker or how powerful negative thinking is in your life, and then we will go over your results.

Are you a Negative Thinker?

1. You just found out that you did not get a job that you interviewed for and really wanted. How do you react?

a) You assume that you are not worthy of the job, and should never have applied.

b) You are disappointed, but you recognize you tried your best, and hope for the best in the future.

2. THE HAIRDRESSER has cut your hair shorter than you'd like it or made some other mistake. How do you react?

a) You think that you are ugly and that the mistake must have been your fault.

b) You're upset, but you realize that your hair will grow back before you know it.

3. YOU REALIZE you made some sort of mistake in your education. What is your reaction?

a) You think you deserve to suffer for your mistake.

b) You realize you made a mistake, but you make the best of it and take any possible steps to correct it.

4. YOU ARE ABOUT to take an exam. How do you feel?

a) You think you are going to do badly, even though you studied hard.

b) You give yourself credit for the studying you have done, and think you will do well.

5. BE HONEST: overall, do you think you are a positive thinker or a negative thinker?

a) A negative thinker.

b) A positive thinker.

SCORING: THE MORE "A" answers you chose, the more negatively you tend to think. But this is your first positive thinking task. You will learn how to get into the habit of positive thinking in this chapter, and you will do well!

Challenging Negative Thoughts

Resisting and challenging negative thoughts can be very difficult at first; it can take some practice to retrain your brain to think in more positive patterns. Just like everything else in life, our thought patterns become habits. We end up thinking the same types of things all the time. If you always think in negative loops, you will continue to do so until you break the pattern. There is a process, and it will take some time to change the way you think.

1. PAY ATTENTION to your thoughts. If you notice yourself going down a dark thought cycle, write that down in your Worry and Anxiety Journal. If you don't have your Journal with you, save it in your phone. You want to keep a record and notice each time this happens. Before we can start to break the negative thought cycles, we have to be aware of when they occur. You want to train yourself to notice as quickly as possible. If you wait an hour to write it down, then you'll train yourself to experience an hour of negative thought before you take action. That's bad training.

2. KEEP your eyes peeled for negative self-talk. This is when you say to yourself things like, "I can't do it." Anytime you notice a negative thought pattern, keep track of it. Once you begin the pattern of noticing when you're entering a negative thought cycle, you then want to begin challenging those negative thoughts.

The first step is a very simple exercise. Imagine you are your own psychiatrist. There are two of you in a room. Transfer your role to that of the psychiatrist; you are sitting in the chair listening to this other version of you describe the thoughts that they are having. By creating this space between you and these thoughts you can be more objective. When you notice your own thoughts in someone else's head, do they seem logical or do they seem very far away from reality?

3. AFTER NOTICING, disconnect reality from negative thoughts and look at an alternative perspective. For example, you're driving to work, someone cuts you off, they slam their car in front of you, and now you're stressed out. This is something everyone's experienced. Your first thought is, "That person cut me off because they think they're better than me," or you think, "I'm not as good as them," especially if their car is more expensive, and we begin to go down the pattern. We always assume it's intentional. But what if something else is happening? What if they are driving their kid to the hospital? What if they are distracted by one of a million other things? Their phone rang, they are going through a rough divorce, they just got fired, they just got bad news, or they lost a loved one.

Look at all these other alternative causes that can result in the exact same action, and none of them is about you. Out of the millions of reasons that someone could cut you off, only one might be intentional and personal. All of the other reasons are not about you. Apply the same logic every time you start to have a negative thought pattern. Every time you think that you have been passed over for a promotion, or someone is playing games, or something bad is coming your way, imagine yourself as the psychiatrist and imagine the advice and alternative possibilities you can give to your imaginary client.

4. PUSH back these negative thoughts and break the loop by putting it into perspective. In the grand scheme of things, is it really a big deal if someone cut you off? There are so many worse things that could happen. Bad things happen all the time. All you have to do is turn on any news channel; they only report bad stuff. If you are not in a war zone, you are not starving, and you are not on fire, then you're doing pretty well. You're beating out a lot of the population just by having

those three things in your favor. Sometimes, we get so caught up in our own heads and our own narcissism that we forget that we have it pretty good.

5. Look for the silver lining or a way to gain from the experience. This is one of the most challenging steps, but it becomes very powerful. A perfect example of this technique in action is the double worry I shared earlier. Once you start worrying about something, it probably won't happen. That's a wonderful silver lining.

When we can find positive results for negative thought patterns, it breaks those loops and takes away their power. Every time you have a negative thought, learn from it and say, "When I have negative thoughts, I become a stronger person." You know those negative thoughts aren't trying to destroy you. They are actually helping you.

Challenging Negative Thinking Exercise

In this exercise, I'm going to take you through a couple of questions and a few scenarios. For each scenario, you're going to select the solution that you think would be the most constructive and helpful in the fight against negative thinking. Our goal is to foster positive thinking.

Write a summary and your answer for each of these questions in your Worry and Anxiety Journal.

1. Mary realizes she did not prepare for the right job interview questions. She finds out that she didn't get the job. She assumes that this result was all because she did not prepare properly, and she is being hard on herself. Which of the approaches below would challenge her negative thinking?

a) Mary should learn from this experience and move on. She'll be ready for the next interview!

b) Mary should avoid interviews for similar jobs in the future.

2. JENNIFER just started at college, and she does not feel like she belongs in her classes. Which of the below approaches would challenge her negative thinking?

a) Jennifer should look at her thoughts objectively and examine how realistic she is being.

b) Jennifer should drop one of her classes.

3. MARGARET HATES her wardrobe and feels awkward because she can't afford to replace her clothes. She thinks people judge her negatively. Which of the below approaches would challenge her negative thinking?

a) Margaret should put the situation into perspective and look at the big picture.

b) Margaret should find a way to buy new clothes, no matter what.

4. JAMES IS HAVING a hard time feeling like he fits in at work and finding his niche. He assumes that no one likes him. Which of the below would challenge his negative thinking?

a) James should consider different explanations in an objective manner.

b) James should worry about losing his job.

5. MAX IS TRYING to lose weight. He just realized he's gained three pounds. He is being very hard on himself. Which of the below would challenge his negative thinking?

a) Max should put the situation into perspective and keep working towards his goal.

b) Max should just give up on his goal.

SCORING: IF YOU CHOSE A LOT OF "A" answers, great work! The "a" answers indicate good tactics for challenging the negative thoughts involved.

Reflection Questions

Write down your answers to these reflection questions in your Worry and Anxiety Journal.

Look at the strategies that we discussed for combating negative thinking. Have you ever used any of these strategies in the past? Can you see how these strategies will help you in the future? Have you tried implementing them since reading the section?

The next time you have a negative thought, practice with these exercises and see what happens. Write down in your Journal your experience and how successfully if you were, the results you faced, and any challenges you discovered.

Did you recognize yourself in any of the scenarios we just discussed? Did any of them sound a little familiar? Write down the moments you have experienced that were similar to these.

How do you feel after completing the exercises and quizzes in the section? Do you think you understand yourself a little better? Do you feel more prepared for dealing with negative thoughts? Are you having negative thoughts about the section, such as, "This won't work for me." Write down your honest feelings and emotions in your Journal.

5

———

THE HELPFULNESS OF MINDFULNESS

Mindfulness, as we discussed earlier, is the ability to live absolutely and totally in the moment; in the "right now." It is when we are totally focused on what we're doing, and we are not distracted by the past or the future. As you live more and more in the moment, your mindfulness will become stronger. This is a skill you can develop and improve. A technique for improving your mindfulness is to focus on your physicality – your body and your breathing. This is why meditation and yoga are effective techniques; they force you to focus on exactly what your body is doing, and you're so busy doing it, that you don't have time to worry.

As we begin to develop your mindfulness ability, we want to start with the baseline. Let's see how strong your mindfulness is right now. Please complete the mindfulness quiz below.

Mindfulness Assessment

1. How difficult is it for you to be in a state of complete mindfulness?
   a) Easy or quite easy.
   b) Extremely difficult or seemingly impossible.

2. How aware are you of the state of your own mind and body?
    a) Generally aware or quite aware.
    b) Not much aware or not aware at all.

3. How easy do you find it to fall into a meditative, completely relaxed state?
    a) Easy or quite easy.
    b) Difficult.

4. How easy do you find it to monitor your thinking?
    a) Quite easy.
    b) Difficult.

Scoring: The more "a" answers you chose, the stronger your level of mindfulness. But whatever you do, don't think negatively! Simply be aware that you need to improve your level of mindfulness and work towards doing so.

Mindful Meditation

I put together a very simple mindful meditation exercise that will help you to control your anxiety. The more you practice this exercise, the stronger your sense of mindfulness will become, and the harder it will be for worry and anxiety to break into your mind.

Step 1. Sit in a chair with your feet flat on the floor and your knees higher than your bum.

Step 2. Ensure that your posture is perfect. Make sure that the very bottom of the spine is curved.

STEP 3. FOCUS on your breathing. Feel the mechanics of each breath; notice as you breathe in, hold for a moment, and then breathe out. Breathing is an unconscious habit; we are so used to breathing, that we forget the actual experience. How does each breath feel as is comes in and provides your lungs with oxygen and energy for your bloodstream? How does each breath feel as your diaphragm pushes it out through your nose and mouth, releasing carbon dioxide back into the universe?

STEP 4. CLEAR your mind of all thoughts other than the moment you're in right now; focus on your senses. How does your skin feel? How does your hair feel? How does each breath feel as it enters and leaves your body? Can you sense your heartbeat? Follow your body from your feet to your head and just notice each set of nerves. How do the bottoms of your feet, your toes, and your ankles feel? Slowly make your way up from your shins to your knees, all the way up to the top of your head. Become aware of each feeling. How does your clothing feel on your body? Can you feel the socks in your shoes? If you're wearing a watch or a bracelet, can you feel it against your wrist? Get in touch with your body, and focus on each feeling in this moment.

STEP 5. HOLD THIS POSITION, focusing on your breathing and paying attention to your body for as long as you can. The first time you practice this exercise, you may only last thirty seconds or a few minutes, but if you practice every day or several times a week, you'll be able to last longer and longer. Your ability to live in the "now" without being distracted by thoughts will become stronger. Soon you will be doing five minutes, ten minutes, and even thirty minutes. When your mindfulness is this strong, you can very easily keep worry and anxiety at bay.

Reflection Questions

Record your thoughts on these questions in your Worry and Anxiety Journal.

1. How do you feel about your results on the mindfulness quiz? Are you more or less mindful than you expected?

2. Did you find the meditation exercise helpful? Did you try it or just read it and skipped right past the section? If you skipped over the mindfulness meditation, please go back and try it, and then write down how you felt before the exercise and how you feel after.

3. Do you feel that the mindfulness exercise helped to lower your anxiety levels? Can you feel a sense of relaxation entering your body?

4. Do you feel that mindfulness could help you become stronger and more aware of the power within you? Do you feel more empowered and more in control of your thought life? Do you like using a physical activity to battle a mental disease?

Rather than fighting worry and anxiety in your mind where they are strong, let's fight them in your body, where they are weak.

6

―――――

CULTIVATING HAPPINESS

Before we can cultivate happiness and grow happiness over unhappiness, we need to come up with a firm definition of the word "happiness." Everyone has their own opinion; in our society happiness has become more of a subjective term. Sociologists are constantly polling people to see which cultures, which societies, and which subgroups are the happiest. They put out reports all the time. This year, men are happier than women. Next year, women are happier than men. Children are happier than adults, and grandparents are the happiest of all. They always put out different results, but at the end of the day, the only way to find out how happy someone is, is to ask them.

Happiness Activity

1. Take a moment to reflect on your definition of happiness. Write down your definition in your Worry and Anxiety Journal. What does happiness mean to you? How can you tell if you're happy? How can you tell if other people are happy? Make a list of all the words, activities, or things that you associate with happiness: places, people, activities, or any other element of life gives you joy. If you're religious, you

may get a great deal of happiness from there. If you're an athlete, you may get a great deal of happiness from participating in your sport. Whatever you enjoy doing, whatever puts a smile on your face, add to that list.

2. WRITE A POEM ABOUT HAPPINESS. It can be short or long enough to rhyme. Don't panic if you feel like you are terrible at poetry. I feel the same way; the thought of writing a book of poetry and publishing it is very daunting to me. The good news is, no one is going to see your poem; it's just for you. Take this chance to be creative and write down a few lines about how you feel when you're happy or what happiness means to you.

3. IN YOUR JOURNAL, beneath your poem, draw a picture that represents happiness. I might draw a picture of snowboarding at the top of a mountain, surfing an amazing wave, or perhaps a picture with my children. These are all things that represent happiness to me.

4. CREATE a collage of what represents happiness for you. This was one of my favorite activities as a child; unfortunately, with the advent of technology, we don't do it very often now. Cut out pictures from magazines and glue them altogether in a collage inside your Worry and Anxiety Journal. Even better, put the collage on the piece of poster board and tape it to the wall in your bathroom or bedroom. Put it where you can see it all the time, to remind you of the things that make you feel happy. Having a happiness reminder around all the time is a wonderful reflection.

YOU HAVE NOW GONE through four happiness activities. Let's go back and think about your definition of happiness. Try to be precise. Can you define happiness in just a couple of words or one sentence, or do you need a whole paragraph?

Now that we've talked about your happiness, let's talk about ways to cultivate happiness and help you become a happier person.

Ways to Cultivate Happiness

1. The first way to cultivate happiness is to smile. No matter how sad you're feeling, stand in front of the mirror and force yourself make a big, toothy smile for one full minute; your mood will change. I often practice this exercise myself. It is one of the greatest ways to demonstrate the interrelationship between physiology and psychology. It's hard to be sad on the inside if you're happy on the outside; your body will go into synchronicity. I bet that earlier in this chapter, when we talked about how to tell if someone is happy, smiling was on your list. It's not just a way to tell strangers you're happy; it's a way to tell yourself that you're happy.

2. CULTIVATE HAPPINESS WITH LAUGHTER. It's hard to laugh angrily. Yes, you can laugh evilly like a villain in a movie, but even when I do that with my darkest and most malevolent of laughs, it makes me happy because it's so silly and fun. There are an infinite number of studies demonstrating that people who laugh more are happier. Children laugh more than adults; that's why children are happier.

As adults, we get very serious, and we feel like we are not allowed to laugh anymore. One of the greatest joys in my life is spending time with my children, watching cartoons, television shows and movies that I thought were very funny when I was a child. Now, I can laugh along with my children. It is very easy to be happy when someone else is guiding you through laughter.

3. SIMPLIFY YOUR LIFE. Often, we feel worry and mental anguish because we are trying to do too many things at once. We have too

many obligations or too many stresses, or we are being pulled in too many directions. Maybe you own too many possessions, and you're trying to maintain your house because it always feels cluttered and overwhelming. That is a very common cause of anxiety in our culture; we become afraid to throw things away because, "What if I need it someday?" That is the ultimate sign that you are not living in the moment. You worry about something that might happen so far in the future that you can't even put a timeframe on it.

4. STOP COMPARING yourself to others. Everyone has strengths and weaknesses, and everyone has flaws and areas where they excel. My life is not perfect. I appreciate you reading this book and following me along this journey. I have some very good things in my life, but I'm not winning in every category. I don't know anyone who's doing 100 percent in every category. As soon as you're healthy, you run into money problems. As soon as your money problems are sorted, you start to have relationship problems. As you have those sorted, then your friend starts acting weird, or someone outside your family gets sick.

There's always something negative; there will always stress. It would be great if we could make stress and worry disappeared completely, but that is not possible. Instead of pursuing something that's artificial and imaginary, we can seek the positive instead. Stress strengthens us; the experience of life improves our character and makes us better people. It makes us smarter and helps us to become stronger. When we see the positive in these challenges, that's when we are focused in the right area.

When we compare ourselves to other people, we often ignore their struggles. People who see my success in business and see that I live on a tropical island think that I got here as if by magic, completely unaware of or ignoring the fact that I slept on a couch for a year and a half after I lost my job to try to learn how to start a business.

They missed the struggle because they only see the "now." When someone looks at you today, they only see today's "you;" they have no idea what your life was like yesterday. When you compare yourself to other people, you are completely ignoring their struggles and their challenges. You don't know the whole story, so the comparison is ineffective and a waste of time.

5. Live a life that is meaningful and authentic. Don't invest your time in activities or relationships that don't mean anything to you. So often, we feel this pressure to do things that we don't want to. We end up going to events we don't want to go to, in hopes that people we don't want to be friends with will respect us. We are so busy thinking what of what other people think that we don't do what we want for ourselves. As much as you may admire that I live on a tropical island, most my friends told me that I was a fool for wanting to live here. Most of the advice from my circle of friends, associates, and business partners was negative; they were against it.

I'm living a life that's authentic, and I'm living my dream. I've had friends come to visit me here, and some of them hated it; this is not the right place for everyone to live. It's not authentic for everyone. If you have a career that makes you feel disingenuous or dishonest, maybe you need to look at pivoting.

When I was younger, I worked for one of the largest companies in the world, and my job was extremely dishonest; everyone I worked with was very dishonest. The longer you worked there, the darker your soul became. After I left this company, I had nightmares for two years. My job was to manipulate people into spending money they didn't have on stuff they didn't need and couldn't afford, and then selling them credit cards that they would never pay off. At the time, I thought it was a great job because I was making a great deal of money, but it was tarnishing my soul. I have no regrets about leaving the company.

6. Cultivate a feeling of gratitude. I like to keep a list of the things

I'm grateful for handy. You can have a little laminated list in your wallet, pocket, or purse all the time. It's always ready to pull out whenever you start to feel down. When I'm worried, I quickly read this list and remind myself of the things I'm grateful for; I'll instantly be less worried. You'll find that if you spend five or ten minutes with your gratitude list, you forget what you meant to be worried about. That's how powerful this technique is.

7. Be kind to yourself and support yourself. We're often our own harshest critics. We hold ourselves to the highest of standards and focus so much on our flaws; rather than focusing on the 97 percent you got right, you focus on the 3 percent you got wrong. Go easy on yourself. Holding yourself to artificial standards and standards that we don't apply to other people only leads to disaster.

8. Be proactive about conflict and confrontations. Our first instinct, when we are upset about something, is to avoid confrontation. That means not telling anyone. It always ends up worse. We bottle it up, and of course, we become more anxious, more worried, angrier, more stressed out, and eventually our behavior changes. We don't tell the person what they did wrong, and we stop spending time with them. We let this feeling grow and fester into a monster.

Whenever you feel you're in conflict with someone, say something as soon as possible. If someone stole your idea, say, "I felt like that was my idea." You may discover that the person says, "Yeah, I steal ideas all the time." In which case now, at least, you know, and you can take proactive actions to deal with that problem. Sometimes they'll say, "You're right. I'm sorry, I forgot where I got that idea. I was working so hard that I mixed things up. I'll give you credit next time." You'll find that ninety-nine percent of people fall into that category. Most people are not intentionally malicious, and when we tell them about a problem early, the problem disappears before it enters your worry life.

9. THINK REALISTICALLY. Sometimes you hold yourself to unrealistic standards or expect things to happen that are beyond the norm. Sometimes we look at other people accomplish things early in life, and we hold ourselves to these impossible standards. It is easy to look at what Jimi Hendrix, Tupac Shakur or James Dean accomplished, and none of them even made it to thirty. At thirty-six, I haven't done nearly as much as those guys did. I can compare myself to them and call myself a loser. James Dean only made three movies, and everyone still knows his name. Thinking that way is not realistic; he's an outlier. And guess what, I'd much rather live to one hundred than burn so bright that I burn out my twenties.

Why compare yourself to the most successful person in the world? You don't have to compare yourself to the best. If you create unrealistic standards, you will never hit them, and it is a waste of time. Focus on achievable and measurable goals, and you will accomplish great things.

10. I can't say this enough: live in your body and live in the exact present moment. Right now, as I write this chapter out on the beach, I'm focused on my body on what's happening in front of me. I'm watching the three different boats rock on the waves, and that's really where most of my thought is. Yes, I'm writing this book, reading my notes, and putting this journey together, but I'm still living in the moment with the majority my body. I'm only thinking about what I'm writing right now. I'm not thinking of what I have to do tomorrow or what I did yesterday. I'm not thinking about what we are doing for dinner later tonight. I am totally focused on what I see, what my body is feeling, and what I am writing.

We get so caught up in our minds that we often don't notice what is happening around us. We often miss when people around us are going through a bad time or when they have a really good experience they want to share with us. How many times have you had a moment where your friend wanted to tell you a story but you told your story first, and then you forgot that they wanted to share something? Maybe you have been on the receiving end as well.

I've been in situations where someone wanted to tell me about a silly story from work, and I wanted to talk about how my best friend just died in a car accident. When they finally let me have my turn, of course, they felt incredibly guilty. We are not aware of things, and we make assumptions all the time. Pay attention to the people around you; how do they interact with each other? What are they thinking?

There is a more advanced technique to practice mindfulness that is also more fun. You can do this activity by yourself or with a friend. Go to a coffee shop, a bar, or any busy place where you can sit and watch people. When you see two people sitting together, try to guess whether they are a date, friends, or related. Create imaginary stories. Just watching their behavior and guessing will strengthen your awareness and force you to be in the moment.

11. Be non-judgmental. Not only do we hold ourselves to high standards, but we hold our friends to the same standards too, and if they fall short, we punish them. I have people in my family who suffer from level ten of this problem – the highest level you can get.

My grandmother died alone and friendless because she held everybody to an impossible standard. In her belief system, if you ever did anything wrong, it was an unforgivable sin, and she would never talk to you again for the rest of your life. It didn't matter the infraction. You would never be told your crime.

You could be friends with her for thirty years, but the day you did something wrong, she would never speak to you again, and you would never find out what you did wrong. It's the same as being arrested and convicted without attending the trial; you don't get to face your accuser, you don't even know what your crime is, and they just put you in a prison cell for the rest of your life. This is how my grandmother lived, and this is how she died.

Unfortunately, other people in my family are the same way. Many years ago, a member of my extended family stopped speaking to my side of the family.

One day, their family came to visit my family. This was long before cell phones and pagers, when you could only call house to house. They were driving quite a distance, and unfortunately, when they arrived, my father wasn't home. My father left the house to go buy a special bottle of wine to celebrate their visit, not knowing when they were going to arrive.

When he came back, we had dinner. Then, suddenly, this family member said they had an emergency, and they all left. They didn't speak to my father's side of the family for nearly twenty years after that. Twenty years later, we discovered the sin my father committed was not opening the door. My mother opened the door instead of my father. This small crime was unforgivable. Like my grandmother, this other member of my family will die alone and friendless.

Don't let this happen to you. Don't hold people to unrealistic, imaginary, impossible standards; you're wasting your time. Forgive people; everybody makes mistakes. Remember, worry and anxiety depend on isolating you. If they can convince you to become one of these people who cut everyone off, they have a great deal more power. You give worry and anxiety all the power over you when they're the only two friends you have left in this world.

12. Focus on the positive. Make a list of all the good things in your life. Your accomplishments, the things that make you happy, and the things you're grateful for. Make a second list with the things you want to do. As things move from one list to the other, you can continue looking at that first list and keep it close to your heart. Keep in your wallet. Every time you start to feel worry and anxiety, look at the list again.

Fighting in the mind is difficult. That's where worry and anxiety are strong, but they are completely powerless in the real world. They can't exist outside your body; like a virus that immediately dies when exposed to air. Bring it out of your body into the world, and fight with action and activity. Reading the list, you might think you're thinking, but you are not. You are reading, you are doing an action, and this will crush anxiety.

13. See the good that's in front of you. No matter how old you are, there are amazing adventures waiting for you. There are more things you can still accomplish; your story is not completed. Focus on the decisions you have left, not the decisions behind you. As we get older, it's easy to look at all the things we did wrong.

Maybe you're still thinking about that relationship that ended ten or twenty years ago that you regret. Let go of that. As much as mindfulness is about ignoring the future, it's also about ignoring the past. Don't get caught up in the past or the future.

Activity

For the next week, use all fourteen of the techniques above. Once you've completed your happiness week, once you have cultivated happiness for a full seven days, answer the following reflection questions in your Journal.

1. Do you feel happier overall?

2. What specific moments can you remember where these techniques really worked for you? What was your happiest moment of the week? What was your favorite part of the last seven days?

3. Were there specific moments where you noticed sadness, depression, worry, or anxiety encroaching on your mind and you successfully applied one of these techniques? What did it feel like to experience that success? Do you feel more hopeful now?

4. Which of these techniques work the best for you? Which did you find the most practical and easy to use?

5. Which of these techniques did you find most difficult or challenging? Why do you think that was? How can you overcome that challenge and use these difficult techniques in the future?

6. How skeptical were you about the concept of cultivating happi-

ness at the start of this chapter? Have you changed your mind? Explain.

7. Have you gained any new insights or wisdom through your week of proactive happiness?

Now spend another three weeks cultivating happiness. Invest a full month in this activity. At the end of the month, write down your answer to the following three questions in your Journal.

1. How happy do you feel right now? How would you rate your happiness now as compared to a month ago?

2. How can you continue to cultivate happiness for the rest of your life? How can you maintain these techniques?

3. How do you feel that using these techniques in raising your happiness level has influenced your levels of worry and anxiety?

7

DISTINGUISHING BETWEEN SOLVABLE AND UNSOLVABLE WORRIES

A very effective stress management technique is to separate your worries into two categories: those you can affect and those you cannot. There are worries and problems that you can solve, and problems that you cannot affect. I often get stressed out and worried when I read and watch the news; all that information is always very negative. I don't have the ability to affect any of it; it's all unsolvable. What's the point of wasting energy and worrying about something you can't actually affect? It's wasted energy.

I want you to take a moment and think about this; every time you have a worry, say to yourself is, "Is this something I can affect? Is this a solvable problem?" If you decide that you cannot affect the problem, then you have to adapt to it and move on. Your worrying won't make a difference, so it is wasted energy. However, if you decide that you can make a difference, then take action.

If someone at work is bothering you, you have to decide if is this a problem you can resolve or not. If you can solve it, talk to the person and ask them to stop doing what they're doing. That is solution number one. If it doesn't work, you go back to your original thought cycle. "I talked to the person, and it didn't work. This person is still bothering me. Is this a solvable problem? Maybe I can talk to my boss." You talk to your boss, and they will either solve the problem or they won't. If the problem is still there, you then have to decide, "Nothing I can do will change the problem. I can't change to another company. My boss won't get involved. I will just have to accept the situation." That's the pattern we go through.

Oftentimes, we worry about things that will never happen. Anything you worry about most likely will never occur. We are terrible predictors of the future. When you begin worrying about something, first realize it is probably never going to happen. Second, look at it and say, "Is this in the realm of reality or is this all imaginary fantasy? Is it something that I will never be able to influence anyway?" Then let it go. Just take that worry and release it like a butterfly into the universe.

Dividing your worries into solvable and unsolvable categories is a critical step in the process of removing stress, anxiety, and worry from your life. You will start to feel more empowered, and you won't treat unequal worries the same. Worrying about taking your driver's test is a practical worry. It's something you can make a difference at if you get a little worried: you study more, you prepare more, and you are more likely to pass the exam. On the contrary, when it comes to elections, we only have one vote and nothing else you do matters. There's no point in worrying about that. Focus your worry where it can be a productive energy. Worry can be valuable when it helps you to prepare for complicated, dangerous, or difficult situations.

Finally, anything from the past is an unsolvable worry. Time machines have not been created yet, and since no one has shown up from the future with a time machine, we know they never will be created. You can't go to the past and change things. Obsessing about something that happened in the past is all wasted energy. I know people who live their entire lives in reference to a single moment, whether it's a great achievement in high school or something really bad that happened when they were younger. They spend the rest of their life blaming everything on this moment, and that moment becomes their highlight reel. For some people it is positive, for some it's negative, but they're all living in the past, and much of their energy is wasted.

Worry doesn't have to be a negative energy; it can be a positive or useful energy. It can help you prepare for critical situations. Don't waste your energy on things you cannot solve. Don't waste it on the past. You're knocking on a door that will never open. The energy in your body and mind should be dedicated to making the absolute most out of every single moment. Live in the right now, not yesterday, not tomorrow.

Hypothetical worries about the future are unsolvable as well. "What will I do if there's an alien invasion? What will I do if there's an ice age? What will I do if this or that happens?" If you are preparing for disaster, and you're stockpiling food in the basement and learning how to survive in the wilderness, that's fine, because you're actually doing something. You are turning that worry into positive energy and developing a skill.

Let's go through some specific examples of solvable and unsolvable worries together now.

Examples of solvable worries

1. You worry that you might have chosen the wrong major in college. You are taking the wrong classes. Most people who go to college experience this worry. I certainly went through this worry; I changed majors five times in my first year and a half at university. I wanted to be a computer programmer until I realized that the computer program at my school was abysmal. I wanted to learn about building websites and programs, and they were teaching me techniques that were basically early 1980s computer programming – a total waste. Nothing on the course was of any value, so I changed my major. This is a solvable worry because you can take action to change it.

2. You worry about your health and weight all the time. You know that overweight people and people who smoke don't live as long, and

you're worried that you won't be there for your kids and your grand-kids. This is a solvable worry; you can take action. This is a worry that comes into my mind all the time now that I have children, and is the reason that I'm constantly spending time with them, eating healthier, and exercising. It is the reason I don't smoke anymore. You can take actions to solve the worry. I don't worry about those things anymore. I know that I'm in much better health than I was three or four years ago because I took action.

3. YOU WORRY that you're not keeping up with your professional knowledge. They say that most physicists come up with their greatest and most brilliant ideas before they turn thirty. That's why most winners of the Nobel Prize are young; after thirty, they get set in their ways, and they see things a certain way, and a lot of the way they see math in the universe gets in stone. This is a common worry throughout many professional fields. Maybe you are an older doctor, and you don't know that every new modern Madison Avenue technique. There is always someone younger who knows more than you. This is a solvable worry; you can get a tutor to help you. You can take night classes or study online. You can read more books.

There are a lot of actions you can take to stay cutting-edge with technology, information, and research in your field. If you worry that you don't exercise your mind enough, buy books of trivia; you can start doing sudoku, or you can get into Mad Libs if you want to exercise your linguistic mind. There are loads of games, night schools, and classes you can take to help you exercise and strengthen your mind.

IF YOU KNOW that you don't eat healthy, that's easily solved by eating healthier. Change your diet, change the decisions you make every day, and the worry goes away. If you're worried that you're not assertive enough at work, that's a common worry; we are worried that people are walking all over us, or take advantage of us, or don't take us seriously enough because we're not assertive enough. The loudest person gets the promotion, rather than the most qualified. It seems like many businesses operate that way.

When you get passed over for a promotion, when you get skipped over for something you deserve and work hard for, you can take more action than just saying, "Become more assertive." You can go and do things that help you become more assertive. You can join a military exercise boot camp program where you get trained by a drill sergeant who toughens you up as part of the program. You can take classes on being more confident and assertive. You can use the exercises from this book and from my course on confidence to become more confident. All these things will help you become more assertive. All the problems from this list are solvable problems; you can take action to make a difference.

In your Worry and Anxiety Journal, write down your own solution to each of these problems. How is each of these worries solvable in your opinion? Just write down one or two sentences so we can solidify that these are solvable worries.

Examples of unsolvable worries

1. You are worried that people thought the dress you wore to the event last night was ridiculous. You were under-dressed or overdressed. This is an unsolvable worry, because it's in the past and we cannot change the past.

2. You worry that you wasted the first two years of college on the wrong major. All that time you could have spent better doing other things is lost. Now you think about it all the time with regret. This too is an unsolvable worry because it is in the past. Worrying about the past is such a waste. We can't touch it. There are many things that would have been better experiences for me, had they been different. But I never think about them because I'm living in the "now" and not in the "fifteen years ago."

3. YOU ARE WORRIED that you will come down with the flu on your honeymoon or your dream vacation. You worry that something will go wrong – you will get sick on the airplane, and you'll ruin the whole trip by being sick. Worrying about a future that is just hypothetical and hasn't happened is such a waste of your energy. You can't solve this; you can't prevent yourself from getting a cold.

You can take all the medicines you want, but if you don't protect yourself from the exact right cold viruses on the plane that day, all of that preparation won't do anything. In fact, being worried and stressed out weakens your immune system and makes you more likely to get sick. You might say to yourself, "Well, I worried and I got the cold. Now I feel justified." But your worry caused the cold, so don't feel justified because you made yourself sick, you made your life worse. An unsolvable worry hasn't happened yet.

4. YOU WORRY that someone you care about will have an accident, get sick, or move away. This is a common worry, and it's a favorite place for worriers to dwell because you're worried about something on which you have no control, and therefore nobody can ever tell you to stop worrying about it. No one can prove that nothing bad will ever happen in the future. Bad things do happen, but the bad things we prepare for are not the things that happen. You can worry about one person getting sick, and a different friend will have an accident. All that worrying was on the wrong person and totally wasted. You are wasting your energy. These are all unsolvable worries.

Exercises

Let's do some activities and reflections to begin thinking about how you can use this technique of splitting worries that are solvable and unsolvable. Write down your answers and your reflections in your Worry and Anxiety Journal.

1. FIVE EXAMPLES

Come up with five unsolvable worries and explain why each is unsolvable. I've already shared with you many examples of unsolvable worries. The easiest way to choose unsolvable worries is to look at politics, the news, the past, or far into the future. Come up with five scenarios and then join me in the next activity.

2. INCREASING CONFIDENCE in Your Ability to Deal with Problems

A combination of turning worry hills into mountains and a lack of confidence in your ability to cope lead you to worry about things that are unsolvable. When we combine these two factors, we end up trapped in cycles, worrying about things we cannot control. Read the following case study and answer the questions below it in your Worry and Anxiety Journal.

Mary tends to worry about all sorts of imaginary hypothetical problems that are pretty much impossible. She worries about things that are never going to happen, but these thoughts and worries stress her all the time, and they affect her mental and physical health. They begin to affect her relationships and her life. She even worries about the mistakes she made in the past, and she dwells on them. She worries about things that could happen at work that could cause her to lose her job. She worries about walking into a meeting and spilling coffee on her boss and immediately being fired.

1. How would improving Mary's level of confidence help her to deal with her worries?

2. If you were Mary's friend, psychiatrist, or counselor, what advice would you give her?

3. How would improving Mary's belief in her ability to cope help her to overcome these challenges?

4. How would improving her tolerance for uncertainty help Mary?

Reflection Questions

Many people are pleasantly surprised at how effective simple solutions are for dealing with worry and anxiety. Sometimes, simply realizing you can't affect the problem, helps you to release that worry into the world and let it go from your mind. However, with some of those thoughts, it happens that you just can't get them out of your mind. You just can't get that voice to go quiet, but remember that worrying is just a thought. You have control over your thoughts; you have the ability to control your thought life both with physical action and through proactive thinking. In this world, you are only in control of two things: how you feel and what you do. As long as you maintain that control, you can push away worry, and it will have no dominion over you.

Think about how powerful you are. The next time a worrying thought enters your mind, I want you to carefully examine your reaction. How does it affect your thoughts, your focus, and your body? Do you start to sweat or feel cold? Is a reaction to this worry helping or hurting the problem? Is the worry making it worse?

Learn to separate yourself from the thought. Extraneous thoughts flow through my mind all the time, but they mean nothing; they come through, and then they disappear. They are not real. Let these worries and negative thoughts flow through your mind, but don't let them take up residence. Ignore them, reject them, do not let them form an attachment within you. After you practice this technique a few times, write down your experience in your Worry and Anxiety Journal. Continue to track how your overall sense of worry and anxiety is changing as you progress and truly change your life.

Test: Combating Catastrophic Thinking

Catastrophic thinking means that you tend to assume that the "worst case scenario" will occur, even if there is no rational reason to think this might be the case. Catastrophic thinking is an extremely stressful tendency to have.

Do you tend towards this kind of thinking? Taking the test below will help you get an idea.

1. How often do you tend to jump to the "worst case scenario" in your thinking about future events?
   a) Often or very often.
   b) Not very often or rarely

2. How nervous do you get about unknown situations?
   a) I'm usually fairly or very nervous.
   b) If there is no rational cause for fear or anxiety, I'm usually not nervous.

3. How negative would you say you are in your expectations of day-to-day life?
   a) Negative or very negative.
   b) I'm not usually negative.

4. How often do you worry about terrible things happening to you or the people you love?
   a) Too often.
   b) Never.

5. I worry about things that never happen.
   a) True.
   b) False.

Scoring: The more "a" answers you chose, the more likely it is that you tend towards catastrophic thinking.

One of the best ways to deal with catastrophic thinking is to rationally focus on how likely it is that the worst will actually happen. When thinking about this question, you need to make sure that you are being logical in every step of the process.

Exercise: Fostering Clear Thinking

Sometimes, we're caught up in the moment, and we can't decide whether a worry is solvable or unsolvable because we're in the midst of emotional turmoil. We are so distracted by what we're experiencing that we can't be objective and get to a space of clear thinking. In order to strengthen your ability to get to a place of clear thinking, you can use techniques such as mindfulness, acceptance, and looking at things in perspective.

In your Worry and Anxiety Journal, write down several techniques that you can use to take a step back and foster clear thinking. I have shared many techniques throughout this book and many mental exercises that I use. Now try to come up with your own mental exercise. What is something you can do to move one step away from the problem? I've talked about my technique of imagining I am my own counselor several times. Develop your own technique and then try it out and write your results in your Journal.

Reflection Questions

In your Worry and Anxiety Journal, write your responses to the following three questions.

1. Do you feel like you are a clear thinker?

2. What blocks your ability to think clearly? What is the primary source of your distraction?

3. How do you feel that clear thinking can improve your life? How can clear thinking help you to combat stress and anxiety?

Exercise: Two-Sided Chart Exercise

Brainstorm some sources of anxiety or potential hypothetical anxieties in your life and then create a two-sided list. On one side, you are going to put down all the unsolvable causes of anxiety. On the other side, we are going to list the anxieties and worries that you can affect or change.

Once you've completed the chart, please spend at least ten or fifteen minutes working on this exercise. Write down a reflection on how you feel and what you learned from this chart. Were there any surprising results? Were there a couple of unsolvable anxiety scenarios that you've always considered solvable? These can take up a lot of your thought life until you realize there's nothing you can do.

Additionally, what are some action steps you can take about the solvable worries to help make them go away? What is one of the sources of anxiety that is most actionable – something you can fix very quickly, something that you could even affect today or tomorrow? If you have one, reflect on this particular anxiety and how you can solve it as quickly as possible, and then take that action.

Write down each step of this process in your Journal and note down what you can do to change. Write down what happens after you take that action, then take a moment and look at one of those anxieties that you cannot change. How does realizing that this anxiety is unsolvable make you feel? Are you still going to invest thought energy into an unsolvable worry that you cannot affect? Or are you feeling a little bit freer after finishing this chapter and these exercises?

8

———

BUILDING UP YOUR TOLERANCE FOR UNCERTAINTY

We live in a world where the future feels very uncertain. Every time I turn on the news, I find out about a new disease or another new potential war. If you let these thoughts into your head, they will occupy you for the rest of the day. The future is uncertain, it is not written, and it will always be uncertain. If you can strengthen your tolerance for uncertainty, then these anxiety levels will diminish.

We have to accept the things we cannot change and the things we cannot predict. One of the ways that uncertainty begins to affect your mind is through "what if" thinking. We begin to develop more and more scenarios. When I was younger, I remember a big scare about spontaneous combustion (that is you might be sitting in a chair watching TV, and your body would simply explode).

Everyone was worried about it for a while, but when was the last time you heard someone talk about spontaneous combustion? No one thinks about that anymore. Then everyone was worried about alien abductions; you would always hear stories of people abducted by aliens. Now that every single phone on the planet has a camera, every person is their own paparazzo. We don't hear about alien abductions anymore. It turned out all these "what ifs" they didn't exist at all, and millions of people invested a great deal of emotional energy in unlikely scenarios.

Sometimes, you get more practical because we don't have enough faith in ourselves. What if I mess up on a credit card application? What if I can't balance my budget properly? What if I lose my job someday? We can obsess about the future because there are millions of bad things that can happen. I could start listing every "what if" I could think of, but then this book would be millions of pages long.

A lot of "what if" thinking is a sign that your confidence is low. "What if thinking" is your way of saying, "I can't handle it if something happens." That's really what you're saying, "I can't handle it." This lack of confidence in the future is poisoning your present. We can raise your confidence and bring you up to a higher level in your tolerance for uncertainty.

Before you begin to work on your confidence, let's assess your current confidence level.

Self-Confidence Test

1. How nervous do you tend to feel before having to be in unfamiliar circumstances of any kind?
   a) Very nervous.
   b) A little nervous maybe or not nervous at all.

2. How COMFORTABLE do you feel with activities like public speaking?
   a) Not very comfortable. I'm usually extremely nervous.
   b) I'm usually fairly comfortable or very comfortable.

3. WHEN YOU have a job interview, how secure do you feel in your possible success?
   a) I feel I don't have much of a chance, even if I'm very well-qualified.
   b) I feel I have an excellent chance of success.

4. Do you ever feel inadequate in any way?
   a) Yes, I often do.
   b) Not usually or never.

5. Do you see yourself as a leader?
   a) No.
   b) Yes.

6. How easy do you find it to express opinions that are different from those of others?
   a) I usually find it difficult to do this.
   b) I usually find it easy to do this.

Scoring: The more "a" answers you chose, the lower your self-confidence currently appears to be. But don't worry! We will go through ideas for how to increase your self-confidence below.

Ways to Improve Your Self-Confidence

I have a list of ten techniques you can use to improve and build your self-confidence. Before we even get to that list, I want to take you through very practical exercise that is unbelievably powerful. The only way "what ifs" work is if we have a poor memory. If we forget the past. You surely have lots of bad things that happened to you, lots of surprises and unexpected scenarios. You endured, and you're still here; you're still walking, you're still talking, you're still alive.

Your ability to endure uncertainty and to handle unexpected and dramatic situations is why you're still here. You're stronger than you realize.

Sit down for a moment and write down at least ten bad things that happened to you and how you were able to adapt to the situation. We often get caught up in these thoughts. "I can't handle if that happens. What if someone in my family gets sick?" But when it happens you deal with it. "What if there is a car accident?" But when it happens you fix it. "What if I lose my job?" And you handle that too.

You are a very powerful person, and you have handled really tough situations in the past. If they happen again in the future, you can still handle them. Write your list in your Journal – make an extensive list of the challenges you have faced and overcome; list the things that made you stronger. Make a tiny laminated copy and shove in your wallet, so whenever you're in a situation where you go, "Oh I don't know if I can handle that," you pull it out and go, "Wait, I have physical evidence that proves I can handle difficult situations!" When it's a thought versus a piece of evidence in your hand, that evidence in your hand will always win. Your list will crush those "what if" thoughts because you have proven that you can handle it if that happens.

Now let's get to my powerful list of ten more techniques.

1. ACKNOWLEDGE your positive attributes and your accomplishments in life. There are many things about you that are great and wonderful. In addition to overcoming challenges, you have skills and assets, things that you're good at, contests you have won, people you've helped, and kindnesses done. It's about time you took credit for the good things in your life and stop focusing on the bad. If you make a list of all the great things, every time you start to worry about something that you're not good enough at, you can look at your list and go, "Here are some of the things I am good enough for." With your list, you have no time to dwell on your negative thoughts because you get too distracted by positive thoughts. They fill up your thought life.

We can only think about five to seven things at a time. Once you try to hold more than seven thoughts in your head, you lose one of the earlier ones. As long as your list contains more than seven items, you'll have cleared your mind of the negative, and you will only have positive thoughts in there. You will have pushed away everything negative.

2. MAKE a point of stepping outside your comfort zone. It's fine to have areas in life where we are comfortable, but if we don't push ourselves further, we don't grow. If we don't grow, we become stagnant. We don't try things because we believe we'll fail. When you try something new, whether you fail or not, you become more confident. There are a lot of things that I tried and failed at, but I feel more confident because actually experiencing failure is so much easier than the thought was. There's that old saying, "A hero dies once, but a coward dies a thousand times."

There are a lot of things that I'm afraid of. I am afraid of heights, but my fear has not stopped me from experiencing things. I've done mountain climbing and cliff diving, and I'm no longer afraid of heights at that level because I know I can survive them. I know I can climb mountains and free climb small cliffs, but I've never jumped out of an airplane. My fear has diminished because I pushed myself out of my comfort zone. Sometimes, you just need to be reminded that you're capable of learning, growing, and handling things that are a little bit tougher than you thought.

3. STOP OBSESSING about what other people think about you. Remember: you have control over what you do and how you feel; do not give that power to other people. This is especially a problem when you are single. Sometimes, a man will talk to a woman, and after two minutes she'll go, "Not interested." He'll walk away with his tail between his legs, ready to cry.

Why would you let a person judge the totality of your value as a human in two minutes? That's not nearly enough time to get to know you. It's not even a full commercial break. Stop giving power to other people. What other people think doesn't matter. Other people aren't thinking about you, they are thinking about themselves.

4. BE TRUE TO YOURSELF. You need to have a sense of authenticity and integrity, so that your actions are in alignment with your beliefs. If you do things you do not believe in, you will constantly damage your sense of self-belief. We have all heard about scientists who work for large companies and put out garbage reports. More and more, we're discovering that the majority of papers published in scientific journals did not follow the scientific method, were not actually peer-reviewed, and most of the research is garbage. In fact, the majority of the articles published are funded by large corporations that have a vested interest in the results. Many scientists have sold their integrity.

If you're doing something you don't believe in, it will haunt you. When I was working for a very large company doing something I didn't believe in, even after quitting, I had nightmares for two years, and everyone I worked with there had a damaged personality. The company was built on a lack of integrity from the top down. Everything inside the company was about treating people poorly and getting away with it. There are a lot of companies built this way.

It's not about what's right and wrong. It's about making as much money as you can and getting away with it. For a while you make some good money, but it begins to affect your thought life and poison you. If you have no sense of morality or you're a sociopath, then this is a great career, and you can continue to do it because you have no sense of integrity.

But if you're a person with integrity and a sense of self, if you're someone who cares about the universe and believes that other people in the world matter, then you may have to leave that career behind and make a little bit less money in order to conquer the worry that is damaging you and hurting your dreams (and sleep).

5. BE KIND TO YOURSELF. It's worth mentioning again: we are often our

own harshest critics. We look in the mirror and say that we are ugly, or stupid, or weak. We should be more confident, but we often take over the voices of our childhood. If you have a stern parent, you hear that voice in your head all the time, even when they are not there.

Stop doing that; stop hurting yourself and start believing in yourself. You deserve a little grace – everyone does. People make mistakes and poor decisions. I do it; you do it. We've all done it. Let go of the past and don't be so harsh. It is okay to learn from your mistakes, but don't punish yourself. You don't deserve it, and it doesn't help.

6. WORK ON YOUR SELF-AWARENESS. Think about why you're having particular thoughts. We want to look at one level deeper than our surface thoughts. We talked about self-awareness before. We watch other people try to figure out what they are doing. As you get better at this activity, you can look at other people and say, "Why are they doing that? Why is he talking to her in that way?" As we look deeper, when you have a negative thought or even begin to think, "I stink," you can immediately go, "Why am I having that thought? What is the cause of that thought?" Look at the layer behind it. The more you become aware of the negative thoughts that enter your life and what the causes them, the easier it is to conquer them.

7. USE CONFIDENT BODY LANGUAGE. If you smile, you become happy; if you stand tall, you become confident. There is a direct correlation between your posture and body language and how you feel internally. If you feel a lack of confidence in yourself, you will begin to hunch your shoulders. Maybe you'll keep your hands in your pockets all the time, which is a body language sign of lack of confidence. But if you change your body and walk with your head held high, shoulders back, you will force your mind to become more confident. This is one of the reasons that the military is so strict about posture. The first thing everyone learns is the perfect salute. The military teaches posture because they know that

posture leads to confidence. Soldiers with bad posture don't fight as well.

8. BE ASSERTIVE. You have not because you ask not. Start to express your desires verbally. You don't start by shouting at people; you can simply say the things you want to say, "I'd like you to consider me for the promotion." "Do you have anything on sale today? Do you have any discounts?" Recently, I talked to a friend of a friend, who has a course I'm interested in. I asked them for a discount, and I said, "Someone I know said you have a really cool course; I'm interested in that. We have some friends in common, and they speak highly of you. Do you have a price for friends – 'mates' rates,' as they say in England?" In this case, I didn't get the discount, but my result is the same as if I had not asked at all. Why not try? Many times, people go, "Here, just have it. Here is a free log in; we're friends, it's fine."

As you become more assertive, you can start to defend your territory and stand up to people who treat you poorly. This doesn't mean you should fight with strangers all the time. You should choose your battles. I'm not a very confrontational person. Most of the time, I'm very passive about things I don't care about. If someone cuts me in line at the supermarket, I probably don't care. However, when it's time to be assertive – if my wife is sick, or my children are threatened – that's a whole different world. That is something that I care about. I save my assertiveness for the right moments.

You need to pick and choose those right battles that are worth expending energy. There are things that matter and things that don't. As you begin to separate those two categories, you will figure out when it's the right moment to be assertive.

9. LET GO of the past. We have said it a few times, but it's so important. The past does not matter. You cannot change the past; it is no longer relevant. It's a movie that we have already watched. Recently in my life, I decided to not re-watch movies anymore. If I've already

seen it once, I won't watch it again. This is how much I want to divorce myself from the past. Everyone makes mistakes and decisions that they later regret. I have made some decisions in my life that I regret; I said things to people that I wish I could take back, but I can't. Worrying about it makes no difference; feeling guilty about it won't change it.

10. Be confident in your thinking. Create an imaginary version of yourself. You already have the imaginary counselor; now it's time to think of the next version of yourself. I always call my imaginary version of myself "Jonathan 2.0." Jonathan 2.0 is very confident; he knows how to handle every situation. When I'm in a tough situation, I imagine what Jonathan 2.0 would do – the competent, cool, suave, little bit of a bad boy version of me.

I say, "What would Jonathan 2.0 do in the situation?" And I do it. Imagine yourself as this more confident version, and then pretend to be this person. What's amazing is that within six months, you will become version 2.0. You'll be so used to acting as this person that the character will subsume you.

Confidence-Building Exercises

You should complete these exercises in your Worry and Anxiety Journal.

1. EXPAND YOUR COMFORT ZONE.

a) Take a few moments to consider exactly what your comfort zone is. Try to describe the breadth of your comfort zone in words. Name some things that are in your comfort zone and some things that are usually outside of it. Reflect on the borders of your comfort zone.

a) Think of an activity or something else that is generally outside of your comfort zone.

b) Come up with a plan of how you could take part in whatever activity this is.

c) Once you have accomplished stepping outside of your comfort zone in this way, record some reflections and thoughts on your experience. How successful do you feel you were? What could you do to make yourself more successful in your next attempt to step outside of your comfort zone?

2. ACKNOWLEDGE your positive attributes and your accomplishments.

a) Write a list of your positive attributes. Rest assured that there are lots of them! Make sure to fill up at least one page.

b) Write a list of the positive accomplishments you have made in your life. Give yourself the credit you are due!

3. IMPROVE your level of self-awareness.

a) How do you feel at this exact moment? Try to describe your emotional state as clearly as possible.

b) Reflect on how difficult or easy it was for you to recognize and describe your exact emotional state.

4. USE CONFIDENT BODY LANGUAGE.

Keep track of yourself and your body language for a full day. How often did you use confident body language? When did you find it most difficult to do so? Why?

5. BE ASSERTIVE.

a) Brainstorm times where you should have been more assertive in the past, and when you can be more assertive in the future.

b) Come up with a plan for increasing your assertiveness in your daily life.

9

THE POWER OF EXERCISE AND NUTRITION

The food you put in your body affects more than just your physical health; it also affects your mental health. Your brain operates using chemical signals that are sent across your neurons; if we change the chemicals we put in our body, then we can change our results. We've all been in one of those moments where we are feeling down and depressed, and so we decide to eat our depression away with a whole pizza and a tub of ice cream. Then we feel gross afterward. You feel disgusted with yourself, "Oh I am so gross. I can't believe I did that." But then you do it again, "I can't believe I ate a whole pizza. I might as well have another pizza."

Having a weak machine will affect your mental clarity. If I go three days without exercising, depression strikes me like a cobra. I cannot maintain my mental health. When we exercise, we release a lot of that negative energy and tension. Throwing a few punches into a punching bag, lifting weights a few times, or even just exercising releases all the negative energy from your body.

I'm a huge fan of yoga. Every morning, after I record my morning podcasts, I do my daily yoga session. I do it first thing to set my day off right. If I missed two or three days in a row, everything feels out of kilter, and I have to make up for it. If I continue to refuse to exercise, my problems become worse and worse. I have no choice but to live healthier unless I want a mind filled with worry and depression.

There are certain foods which cause more tension and anxiety, and maybe you will recognize a few things that have too large of a position in your current diet; salt, caffeine, sugar, alcohol, and processed foods. All of these contain chemicals that damage your signaling processes.

One of my simple rules for diet is I don't eat any food that was inside a factory. If you go to the supermarket with this rule in your mind, you will discover that you're not allowed to touch most of the things there. You can't eat frozen food; you can't eat anything in a box. When you look at these cardboard boxes, the ingredients are unbelievable. The ingredients for a banana consist of one banana – there are no ingredients! But if you look at ingredients on a package of banana chips, it's horrifying. There are so many chemicals in there. In America, they don't even list all the ingredients – they only have to list most of them. Just making the decision to not eat factory food will dramatically improve your confidence and lower your anxiety.

Foods that Help Assuage Anxiety and Stress

There are certain foods which actually lower anxiety levels because they contain the right types of chemicals. These are foods like turkey, which includes tryptophan. Tryptophan is the chemical that makes you sleepy after you eat turkey; that is why everyone falls asleep after Thanksgiving dinner.

Anything with lots of vitamin B is amazing for your body. Leafy greens, pork, chicken, legumes, nuts, eggs, whole-grain carbohydrates, salmon, high-protein foods, and chamomile tea. There's a reason why when you're feeling anxious they don't offer you that Earl Grey, but you go for the chamomile tea. It relaxes you, and it soothes the soul.

The Benefits of Exercise in Fighting Anxiety and Stress

In addition to eating a little healthier and bringing a few changes to your diet, exercising has consistently been shown to lower anxiety levels. A little exercise and a little change in your diet will really make a difference.

There are many benefits to using exercise to combat stress and anxiety.

1. EXERCISE INCREASES your energy levels. When I was younger, I always thought I shouldn't exercise if I was too tired. "I only have a little bit of energy left, and I don't want to waste it on exercise. I'll have no more energy to get through the day." That's absolutely wrong. When I exercise, I gain more energy. When I finished my morning yoga routine, I am panting, dripping in sweat, and I'm physically exhausted, and yet, twenty minutes later, I feel fully energized, and I have a better day.

2. EXERCISE IMPROVES YOUR OPTIMISM. When you exercise, your body is excited. We are built for a physical life. Our bodies were designed and perfected long before we began living in houses. We are designed for a world of hunters and gatherers. Our bodies are built to run around and do physical things. When your body is happy, your mind is happy. When you exercise, your body pumps endorphins in your brain. These are the brain chemicals of happiness and cheerfulness. We are fighting where we're strong and where anxiety is weak; fighting with your body rather than your mind makes it much easier to push stress and anxiety away.

3. EXERCISE IMPROVES clarity of thinking. When exercising hard, I can't focus on anything other than the moment. All the distractions of yesterday and the thoughts about the future are gone. I can't think

about what I want to do later today; I have to provide total focus in that moment. It boosts your confidence. You feel good about yourself. Nobody exercises and feels bad about themselves. No matter what your physical level is, you can move your body. If you can't run, go for a walk. If you can't walk, do something lighter. Find something you can do and work your way up as your body gets back into balance.

4. Exercise reduces tension. Oftentimes, tension is marked by an increase in blood pressure and a higher pulse. The healthier you become, the lower your resting heart rate and the lower your blood pressure. Those physical manifestations of stress and anxiety will diminish.

5. Exercise improves your self-esteem. After a workout, you feel good about yourself. You did something good, you accomplished it, and you just feel wonderful.

6. Exercise improves your sleep pattern. When we don't burn off the proper amount of energy during the day, we have trouble sleeping at night. There's too much excess energy stored in our body. Too many of the wrong chemicals are out of balance. But when you've had a good exercise session, you'll sleep the best sleep you've had in a very long time.

7. Exercise improves your ability to cope. You begin to have more faith in your body, and you start to think about more scenarios you can handle, "If I need to run, I can run. If I need to run up a flight of stairs, I can. If I need to grab my kids and run away from a fire, now I can." Your belief in yourself begins to increase as your ability to do things increases.

There are certain forms of exercise that are very beneficial: walking, bicycling, yoga, Pilates. Even team sports can be wonderful; exercise doesn't have to be unpleasant. You can find an adult sports league and play kickball or ultimate Frisbee. You can find something that's fun and not stressful; you don't have to worry about getting picked last. Find something where you enjoy the process.

Yoga

Yoga is becoming trendier and trendier, and more and more people practice it. When I was young and single, I loved going to group yoga classes and being surrounded by beautiful yoga ladies, but now that I'm married that doesn't interest me. On my island, there are multiple yoga classes available every day; you have one at sunrise, one at sunset, and anytime in between in five or six different yoga studios. That doesn't work for me. Instead, I start my day by watching a yoga DVD. I do yoga with my wife. My children like to watch, and sometimes they participate; we make it a family activity.

There are lots of different ways you can do yoga, whether you want to do in a group or by yourself. Yoga is good because it's built around a lot of anxiety-reducing techniques. Meditation, controlling your breathing, and focusing on your physicality are a big part of yoga. Yoga is tied directly into your mental focus, experiencing your body, and living in the now.

One of the best ways to dip your toe in the water with yoga is to join a local class. I do recommend starting with a couple of sessions with an instructor so that you can learn the correct positions and movements. Once you've learned all those positions, you can stay in a class or begin to do it on your own. There are beginners' DVDs as well. Find the ones that work for you and the course that works for you.

Pilates

After the trend with yoga, Pilates came on the scene. I believe Pilates was invented a hundred years ago, and it involves a few more machines. Many people in my life, including my mother, are huge believers in Pilates. It's a wonderful exercise for men and women. It's built around flexibility and muscle health, and it's very similar to yoga. It focuses on the same type of strengthening conditioning.

If you have any limitations as far as weight, injuries or joint problems, then Pilates is something I wholeheartedly recommend. It was originally developed for recovering from injury. If you've always thought, "I can't exercise because of these problems," Pilates may be the perfect solution for you.

There are loads of Pilates courses out there, and DVDs and videos you can watch online just like anything else; maybe you want to watch one of those videos before you try a course. Just like with yoga, I recommend starting with someone who can check if you're doing it right, so you don't make any mistakes or risk injury. Just like if you decide to get in the lifting weights, you want to make sure you do each lift properly to avoid injury. Once you have that down, then you don't need help as much.

Your New Exercise Plan

You might be thinking, "Exercise and diet? That sounds wonderful. I am definitely going to start doing that *someday*." Wrong! The time to take action is now. Break out a new notebook and start an Exercise Journal. Here are a few basic minimal guidelines.

Make sure you have ten minutes of exercise built in every day – just ten minutes of getting your heart rate up will make a difference in your life.

Try to mix in multiple forms of exercise. This is very important. I do yoga in the morning to start off my day, and later in the afternoon, after I finish my work sessions, I go outside and do something in the ocean. I pull out the kayak out and put in some time behind those oars. I get on my paddleboard, I go for swim, or I go surfing. I do something physical that works different parts of my body, and each activity is enjoyable in a different way. When I'm out on the water, there's no structure, no timer, and there's no one watching.

You might do something different – maybe you have ten minutes of weightlifting, and then you go play a sport, like kickball, or you join a hiking club or one of those walking photography clubs. Mixing up a few different things will make it easy for you get started.

In your Exercise Journal, create an exercise log. Every day, write down your exercises. Write down what was hard. Track your numbers, and write down how you felt. If you're lifting weights, write down how much weight you lift every time you do it. If you are going for a jog, write down how long you jog for and check your heart rate.

Tracking lots of numbers and statistics also allows you to see your improvement. If you don't keep a log, you will feel like you have not improved and you'll quit. Keeping a journal means protecting the future version of you from quitting too soon.

Warm-up before your exercise and a cool-down afterward. Exercise for twelve or fifteen minutes total, with two minutes to warm up and two or three minutes to cool down after. Over time, you will begin to exercise for longer sessions. You don't have to do marathon sessions.

Most of my yoga DVDs are only twenty-five or thirty-five minutes. I like that they are short. With all the things happening in my life, I don't have two hours in the morning to do all the things I want to start my day with. My children are chomping at the bit to get my attention, so I found something that fits and works for me. It's so intense that at the end of those thirty minutes I have nothing left to give; it totally sucks out all my energy. There are more intense, shorter workouts, and there are a little more casual, longer ones. Both get you the same result in the end. Find the one that's right for you.

Reflection Questions

Commit to exercising at least ten minutes a day for the next month.

In your Worry and Anxiety Journal or your brand-new Exercise Journal, write down your answers to the following questions. Make sure that you answer these questions once a week, as you begin to bring more exercise and a better diet into your life. Answer these questions every week for the next four weeks.

1. Measure your overall anxiety level. Has it gone up or down since you started this exercise routine? Is it higher or lower than last week?

2. How is your self-confidence this week? How has exercising improved your self-confidence?

3. How has your ability to cope with stress changed over the last seven days?

4. Have you found yourself worrying about things you can't change and things that don't matter less?

5. Since you began your entire exercise regime, how has your general sense of happiness and well-being changed?

10

————

DEALING WITH ANXIETY IN YOUR EVERYDAY LIFE

We have covered a lot of ground in this book so far; we've broken down anxiety and stress into their component parts, and we've seen many different techniques you can use to combat these negative forces. However, with so many different techniques, it might feel like too much to try and practice every technique every day; you might feel a little overwhelmed by the idea of changing your diet and exercising more, meditating, doing yoga, and adding all these elements at once. Let's design an action plan you can use in everyday life. Take a look at a few real-life examples and how you can put them into practice.

1. RECOGNIZING UNNECESSARY WORRY. Hannah worried constantly about mistakes she had made in the past. She constantly tormented herself, calling herself stupid and dumb and reliving the mistakes over and over again. Finally, she decided to make a change, and she forgave herself. She realized that, like anyone else, she's not perfect, and she decided to give herself a little grace. She forgave herself and stopped beating herself up so much. She chose to move on with her life, focusing on living in the moment and building her mindfulness

rather than living in the past. Instead of dwelling in the past, she chose to give herself permission to feel joy again.

2. Improving mindfulness. Jack found himself always worried about the future, always wondering what was going to happen next. He could never feel prepared enough for all the different possibilities. He felt like he had no control over his destiny or the path his life was taking. He finally decided to take control of his life and began to focus on mindfulness. He decided to only live in the present and to not think about anything more than three days in the future. Just shortening how far in the future he was willing to worry dramatically changed his life and gave him a new-found sense of peace and freedom. A weight had been taken from his shoulders.

3. Maintaining your exercise plans. Mary got so busy with work and taking care of her family she didn't have any time to exercise. She had so many obligations that exercise always got knocked off the table. She noticed herself moving slower and slower, and she became unhealthy. She decided that small steps are better than no steps and began with exercising just ten minutes a day. She noticed her anxiety levels lowering, even though she was spending more time exercising. She felt like she had more free time throughout the day.

4. Eating healthy. Maxine was addicted to junk food. She needed that jolt of energy from something sweet or salty just to get through the day. Whenever she felt her energy flagging, she would turn to sugar and caffeine. The problem was, the energy never lasted. At most, a candy bar would give her energy for a few hours, and then she would need a soft drink, more coffee, or a bag of chips.

She found herself eating seven or eight snacks throughout the day. She realized that she was chasing a sugar high. The energy bursts never lasted long enough, and she became tired of crashing.

When shifted to eating healthier food instead of processed foods, she found her energy no longer flagged throughout the day. She didn't need a chocolate bar at 10AM. She didn't need a post-lunch snack at 2PM. She was able to get through the day eating healthier and eating less. She began to feel better about her body and her diet; her confidence improved, and her anxiety and worry began to fade away

5. LEARN how to say no. Tracy was a self-confessed people pleaser. She found it hard to say no, even when someone else's request would be a major inconvenience for her. Sometimes, she would accept projects when she was exhausted and had no more energy left. She had nothing left to give, but she continued to push herself harder. Eventually, after a scare at the doctor's office, she realized it was time for change. She couldn't continue to live this way; the stress and anxiety were literally eating her apart from the inside out. She began putting her health first and saying no to all those extraneous projects. Her workload is now more manageable, and her anxiety is beginning to diminish.

6. AVOID UNNECESSARY STRESS. David was always worrying about problems he could never solve. Every morning, to start his day, he'd go to his favorite news website and read every story. He was always worried about environmental, political, and international problems. It felt like the world was turning into hell in a handbasket, and there was nothing he could do about it. He finally realized that all that stress was wasted energy. He was worrying about problems he had no ability to influence. He stopped visiting that website and, in fact, he stopped following the news altogether. That one tiny habit change released him from the stress in his life.

Reflection Questions

Write your answers to the following questions in your Worry and Anxiety Journal.

1. What will be your first steps towards dealing with stress and anxiety in your everyday life?

2. How can you be kinder to yourself?

3. What is a habit that you should change right now to stop bringing stress and anxiety into your life?

Before and After Reflection Activity

Go for a long, relaxing walk, or intensely meditate for at least ten minutes. Both before and after this activity, answer the following questions. At the end of your Journal, you should have two sets of answers. One on the left side of the page, and one on the right side of the page. At the end of this entire exercise, look at your two sets of answers and compare.

1. How much tension do you feel right now?

2. How much of your mental energy is directed towards anxiety and stress? What percentage of your mental bandwidth is thinking about stressful things?

3. On a scale of 1 to 10, rank your self-confidence in this moment.

4. How effective do you feel right now? How capable do you feel of accomplishing the things you want to accomplish?

5. How relaxed you feel?

6. Do you feel in charge of your life right now? How much control do you have over your destiny?

7. Are there areas of your life where you feel you lack control?

11

MOVING ON WITH YOUR LIFE

We covered a lot of ground in this book, and some of this might have gone beyond the scope of what you expected. Perhaps you thought we'd only talk about worry and anxiety. We talked a little bit about depression, a little about self-confidence, and a bit about mindfulness. Try to take a whole-body approach to dealing with worry and anxiety. Not every tactic will be perfect for you.

Out of the dozens of techniques we shared, perhaps you'll find three or four that work for you, and you should focus on them. They give you the results you've always desired. Just because you have a dozen tools, you don't have to use all of them to solve every problem. It's okay to use the ones that are most effective for you.

To see how far you progressed, let's take one final assessment together.

Final Assessment

1. How strong is your self-confidence?
    a) Much stronger than it was than before I read this book.
    b) No stronger than it was before I read this book.

2. How generally in control of your life do you feel?
    a) Much more in control than I did before I started reading this book.
    b) No stronger than I felt before I started reading this book.

3. How solid is your self-esteem now?
    a) Stronger than it was before I started reading this book.
    b) No stronger than it was before I started reading this book.

4. When a worry or anxiety comes into your mind, how good are you at preventing it from affecting you?
    a) Much better than I was before I started reading this book.
    b) No better than I was before I started reading this book.

Scoring: The more "a" answers you chose, the better your improvement in dealing with worry and anxiety. If you chose one or more "b" answer, don't worry! Go back and review the book, and redo whatever exercises you think would benefit you. For some of us, dealing with worry and anxiety can be a longer journey. There's nothing wrong with that! You are more than worth the time and energy it takes!

Here are some reflection questions for you to answer.

Reflection Questions

1. Now that you have an entire toolbox of techniques, tactics, and strategies for dealing with stress and anxiety, what new hopes and plans do you have for your life?

2. What areas do you feel more confident? Do you feel inspired to try new things, learn something new, or even attempt something you've always thought would be too difficult? Is there an activity that's

always been one step away from your bucket list but now you feel ready to give it a try?

3. How would you rate your current level of optimism? Do you feel more optimistic than when you began this journey with me? How do you feel that optimism might help you with future endeavors?

4. On a scale of 1 to 10, how would you rate yourself as a worrier? Has your tendency to worry gone down, or has this book backfired and you worrying is now higher than ever before?

5. Do you find it easier to deal with your worry now you have a stronger understanding of how it works and how you can break it apart into something that you can overcome?

The End of the Road (or the Beginning?)

You've done it – you reached the end of your journey, and I'm very excited! Worry and anxiety can be an overwhelming part of your life, and they certainly were part of my life for a long time. As someone constantly obsessed with disaster, my creative imagination often overwhelmed me with the possible horrible things that could happen to me and the ones I loved. I lived in constant fear of the most irrational and unlikely hypothetical futures.

I know where you were when you started this book because that used to be me, and I know where you are now because you have the same tools that I have – the same tools I use to push worry and anxiety away and turn them into a positive force in my life that I only use when necessary.

I am proud of you for finishing this book and completing this whole journey working your way through the activities. If you're serious about changing your life, I'm serious about helping. But the journey is not complete.

I'm still available to you. If you communicate with me, I'll gladly help you on this journey. If you still feel stress and worry, or if you feel like the techniques in this book weren't enough, I am glad to help you develop some custom techniques that work for you. This is a two-way street; we are on a journey together.

As a reader of one of my books, you're now a valued member of my tribe. The name of my tribe is Serve No Master, and that involves more than just not serving a boss in an office; it also means not letting your emotions master you; not letting some bad emotion determine the path of your life and taking control. You're the only one in charge of your life, and that's what I want for you.

In a few moments, you'll have a chance to turn the last page, and you can decide whether or not to leave a review. If you haven't tried the exercises, if you haven't written anything down in a notebook, then the odds of these techniques working for you are very slim. If you tried everything and they still didn't work, please reach out to me. I would much rather help you overcome your anxiety. Give me a chance to continue to work with you. I'm there for you.

A lot of love, blood, sweat, and tears went into this book. You've done the first half of your job by reading this book. Now it's time for you to take action and change your life. When you implement the activities, use the techniques, and alter your mindset, you'll discover you can wake up with a smile on your face every day, and that is the reason I took the time to write this book.

ONE LAST CHANCE

D id you forget to join us? It's not too late!

ServeNoMaster.com/worrygroup

THANK you for your purchase of *Stop Worry and Anxiety*. As an extra bonus, I want to give you a free gift.

We have a special and amazing group of entrepreneurs and authors who have all been where you are right now.

Having a group of people around you who understand depression, anxiety, and stress is the BEST way to stay the course and overcome your problem.

With our support your success becomes inevitable.

Now that you've read this entire book, we want to congratulate you RIGHT NOW.

Accelerate your success and click the link below to get instant access:

ServeNoMaster.com/worrygroup

FOUND A TYPO?

While every effort goes into ensuring that this book is flawless, it is inevitable that a mistake or two will slip through the cracks.

If you find an error of any kind in this book, please let me know by visiting:

ServeNoMaster.com/typos

I appreciate you taking the time to notify me. This ensures that future readers never have to experience that awful typo. You are making the world a better place.

ABOUT THE AUTHOR

Born in Los Angeles, raised in Nashville, educated in London - Jonathan Green has spent years wandering the globe as his own boss - but it didn't come without a price. Like most people, he struggled through years of working in a vast, unfeeling bureaucracy. And even though he was 'totally crushed' when he got fired, it gave him the chance to reappraise his life and rebuild it from scratch.

Since 2010, he's been making a full-time living on the Internet - helping brick and mortar business owners promote themselves on the Internet, helping men and women find true love, ghostwriting best sellers for some of the biggest publishers in the world and much, much more.

Thanks to smart planning and personal discipline, he was more successful than he could have possibly expected. He traveled the world, helped friends and family, and moved to an island in the South Pacific.

Now he's passing his knowledge onto the rest of the world as host of a weekly podcast that teaches financial independence, networking with the world's most influential people, writing epic stuff online, and traveling the world for cheap.

His hobbies include kayaking, surfing, and building empires. He currently has a loving girlfriend, and two wonderful kids who love the ocean (almost!) as much as he does.

Find out more about Jonathan at:

ServeNoMaster.com

ALSO BY JONATHAN GREEN

Serve No Master Series

Serve No Master

Breaking Orbit

20K a Day

Control Your Fate

Habit of Success Series

PROCRASTINATION

Influence and Persuasion

Overcome Depression

Stop Worrying and Anxiety

Color Away Depression

Love Yourself

ONE LAST THING

Reviews are the lifeblood of any book on Amazon and especially for the independent author. If you would click five stars on your Kindle device or visit this special link at your convenience, that will ensure that I can continue to produce more books. A quick rating or review helps me to support my family and I deeply appreciate it.

Without stars and reviews, you would never have found this book. Please take just thirty seconds of your time to support an independent author by leaving a rating.

Thank you so much!

To leave a review go to ->

https://servenomaster.com/worryreview

Sincerely,
Jonathan Green
ServeNoMaster.com